D0246915

LIFE BEHIND
THE GREAT WALL

JOURNEYS INTO THE PAST

LIFE BEHIND
THE
GREAT WALL

Published by
THE READER'S DIGEST ASSOCIATION LIMITED
London   New York   Sydney
Montreal   Cape Town

IMPERIAL CENTRE   Shades of red dominate a Beijing street of about 1835. Once the world's largest city, the Chinese capital lost its place to the new industrial cities of the West.

DOWN, SPOT!   A pigtailed boy plays with a household dog in an 18th-century painting.

IN THE FIELDS   Peasants gather the rice harvest. Rice is a crop of southern China where most suitable fields are flooded to make paddies and up to three harvests can be gathered in a year.

LIFE BEHIND THE GREAT WALL
Edited and designed by Toucan Books Limited
Written by Christopher and Gila Falkus

First edition copyright © 1996
The Reader's Digest Association Limited,
Berkeley Square House, Berkeley Square, London W1X 6AB

Copyright © 1996
Reader's Digest Association Far East Limited
Philippines copyright © 1996
Reader's Digest Association Far East Limited

All rights reserved
No part of this book may be reproduced, stored in a retrieval system, or transmitted in any form or by any means, electronic, electrostatic, magnetic tape, mechanical, photocopying, recording or otherwise, without permission in writing from the publishers.

® Reader's Digest, The Digest and the Pegasus logo are registered trademarks of The Reader's Digest Association, Inc, of Pleasantville, New York, USA

Printing and binding: Printer Gráfica S.A., Barcelona
Separations: Rodney Howe Limited, London
Paper: Perigord-Condat, France

ISBN 0 276 42130 2

PAGE 1: An early 18th-century illustration shows female workers winding silk.

PAGES 2-3: A drummer beats his instrument and finely robed officials watch as archers take part in a contest.

Front Cover (clockwise from top left): Child visiting grandfather; Chinese merchant; a dinner party; sweet and toy-seller; boxwood pendant with yin and yang and sacred trigram; boy playing with dog; transporting opium; Emperor Pu Yi.

Back Cover (clockwise from top left): A palace courtyard; watering tea plants; interior of a mandarin's house; teapot made for European market; 17th-century portrait of Confucius; the lesson.

Contents

Secret of Long Life According to popular Taoist beliefs, the crane and the pine tree were symbols of longevity – to be achieved by the right spiritual and physical disciplines.

Tao Teapot The character 'shou', represented in this teapot, stood for longevity. Religious, as opposed to the higher-browed philosophical, Taoism involved a belief in magic symbols and cures.

Shanghai Wheelbarrow The Scottish photographer John Thomson captured this scene of a man and woman being pushed along in a rickshaw.

Silk Farm The different members of a family collect silk cocoons and sort them into baskets for taking to market.

THE MIDDLE KINGDOM

China's last imperial dynasty, the Qing, ruled for more than 250 years from 1644 to 1911.

These were years of change for the 'Celestial Empire', encompassing times of both immense prosperity

and seemingly helpless decline. Yet many aspects of everyday life remained true to age-old traditions.

WHEN GEORGE STAUNTON, secretary to Britain's ambassador Lord Macartney, asked the Chinese in 1793 what the population of their empire was, he was proudly informed that it stood at 353 million. The mandarins may have been exaggerating by the odd 50 million – but China's population still amounted to at least a quarter of the human race and was far larger than the population of all the European nations, including Russia, added together.

The imposing size of the population was matched by the vast extent of China's territories. The Communist China of today, covering some 3.7 million sq miles (9.6 million km²), is marginally larger than the United States of America. Two centuries ago China's rulers held sway over an area a fifth as large again. In the extent and variety of its landscape their realm was not a country but a continent, embracing mighty mountain ranges, densely cultivated river valleys, vast windswept wastes and the largest cities on the face of the planet.

Contrasts of environment, from the subtropical to the subpolar, were reflected in contrasts of lifestyle and diet. Rice was the staple of the humid south; wheat grew in the chilly north. Linking the two regions was the world's largest network of natural and man-made waterways. Strikingly different lifestyles among the emperor's subjects included those not only of diligent peasants but also of nomads and tribal hill-peoples numbering millions.

PARADOXES OF POWER AND POLICY

Many Westerners who studied China were confounded by its paradoxes. The Qing dynasty seized power in 1644 and in the subsequent century and a half annexed huge swathes of territory, which more than doubled what they had initially conquered. In that they proved themselves to be outward-looking. Yet the same regime consistently discouraged subjects from migration overseas and tried repeatedly to recall communities that had established themselves throughout South-east Asia.

In matters of technology the Chinese had shown themselves to be extraordinarily creative, inventing silk, paper, porcelain, gunpowder, the wheelbarrow and the mariner's compass, and building immense canals and iron bridges, 1000 years before such projects were attempted in Europe. Yet, by the late 18th century, at the very time that Europe's own technological creativity was leaping ahead, China's

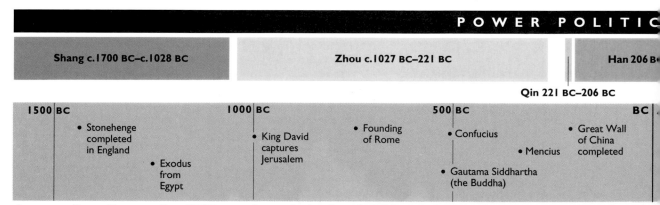

POWER POLITIC

Shang c.1700 BC–c.1028 BC	Zhou c.1027 BC–221 BC	Han 206 B

Qin 221 BC–206 BC

1500 BC	1000 BC	500 BC	BC
• Stonehenge completed in England	• King David captures Jerusalem	• Founding of Rome	• Great Wall of China completed
• Exodus from Egypt		• Confucius	• Mencius
		• Gautama Siddhartha (the Buddha)	

ANCIENT OF DAYS For more than 3500 years the continuing thread of Chinese culture survived the rise and fall of dynasties.

AT HOME A villa harmonising with the landscape sums up the poise and balance of China's ancient civilisation.

had not merely faltered but stagnated. This revealed itself in an astonishing lack of curiosity about Western technology. The fine clocks and guns brought by Lord Macartney as presents for the emperor were dismissed as trivial toys. They were of no significance to the self-sufficient empire which called itself the Middle Kingdom and expected all its surrounding, and by definition, lesser neighbours to acknowledge its inherent supremacy.

Language presented another paradox. A Western traveller who tried to get to grips with 'Chinese' had to grasp that it was not a single language but many. There were at least eight main varieties of Chinese speech, as different from each other as the languages of western Europe, not to mention the tongues spoken by minorities and in frontier regions, such as Tibetan, Uighur (related to Turkish and spoken in the far north-west) or Mongolian.

Chinese speech patterns, moreover, were very different from Western ones, employing variations in tone to establish fundamental differences of meaning. In what became known in the West as Mandarin, the predominant speech of Beijing and the north, the simple particle 'ma', pitched at a high level, meant 'mother' but at a high and rising level meant 'hemp', at a low-falling-rising level 'horse' and at a high-falling level 'scold'. 'Horse slow. Mother scolds horse' therefore fell on uncomprehending ears as 'Ma man. Ma ma ma'. And whereas Mandarin operated on four such tone levels, the dominant speech of the south, subsequently known in the West as Cantonese, used six.

Such linguistic diversity made communication difficult not only between Chinese and foreign visitors but also among the Chinese themselves. As a check against nepotism and other forms of corruption, the custom developed of posting magistrates to districts far away from their place of birth. This meant that in many cases the speech of the ordinary people whose lives they were supposed to

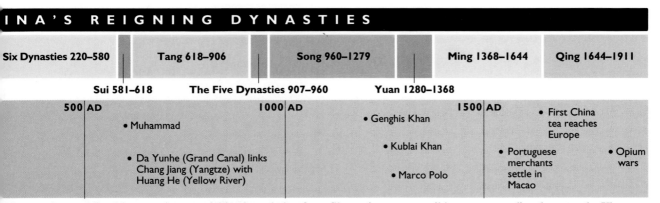

INA'S REIGNING DYNASTIES

| Six Dynasties 220–580 | Tang 618–906 | Song 960–1279 | Ming 1368–1644 | Qing 1644–1911 |

| Sui 581–618 | The Five Dynasties 907–960 | Yuan 1280–1368 |

500 AD	1000 AD	1500 AD
• Muhammad	• Genghis Khan	• First China tea reaches Europe
	• Kublai Khan	• Portuguese merchants settle in Macao	• Opium wars
• Da Yunhe (Grand Canal) links Chang Jiang (Yangtze) with Huang He (Yellow River)	• Marco Polo	

a boasts the world's oldest continuous civilisation, dating from Shang times or possibly an even earlier dynasty, the Xia.

7

regulate was quite unintelligible to them, forcing them to rely on local scribes and constables to act as their interpreters.

These same tongue-tied officials could, however, communicate with their supervisors in the remote capital thanks to their mastery of a written form of the language. This was common to all who had studied the classic writings of the ancient philosopher Confucius (*c.*551-479 BC) and passed through the hierarchy of examinations which made them eligible for office.

NORTHERN BARBARIANS

The supreme paradox of Qing China was that its presiding dynasty was of alien blood and language. The Qing were Manchus, from the wild frontier region of Manchuria. When they seized power these 'northern barbarians' can have numbered no more than 2 million. They were assisted by fierce Mongol allies, and even more by the treachery of certain generals of the tottering Ming regime, China's last native dynasty. But the Manchus' ability to take, conquer, hold and enlarge the empire rested basically on their own fighting prowess.

This they owed to Nurhachi (1559-1626), a warrior chief who had reorganised his tribal society, with the aid of Chinese renegade advisers, into a military machine. He divided his elite forces into four divisions, each with its own flag. These four groups of 'Bannermen' were later expanded to eight and eventually, with the addition of equal numbers of Mongol and Chinese units, to 24. When the conquest of China was complete, garrisons of Bannermen, posted to major cities and key strategic points, were used to police the empire and extend its frontiers.

Although the Qing installed themselves in Beijing in 1644, it took another 40 years to crush the last major resistance to their rule. This resistance was concentrated in the south. Here, especially in the fertile basin of the Chang Jiang (Yangtze Kiang), lay the richest and most populous part of China. But the Qing, like the Ming before them, preferred to base their capital at Beijing in the north, even though it was a long way from the centre of gravity of the empire's core 'Eighteen Provinces' strung out along the coast from the Gulf of Tong-king in the south as far as the border with Korea in the north and

MULTIPLE MANPOWER A Chinese tapestry (above) records a scene from British ambassador Lord Macartney's mission of 1793-4. The scientific instruments were gifts from Macartney. Peasants in 1874 (right) use chain-pumps to draw off river water for irrigation.

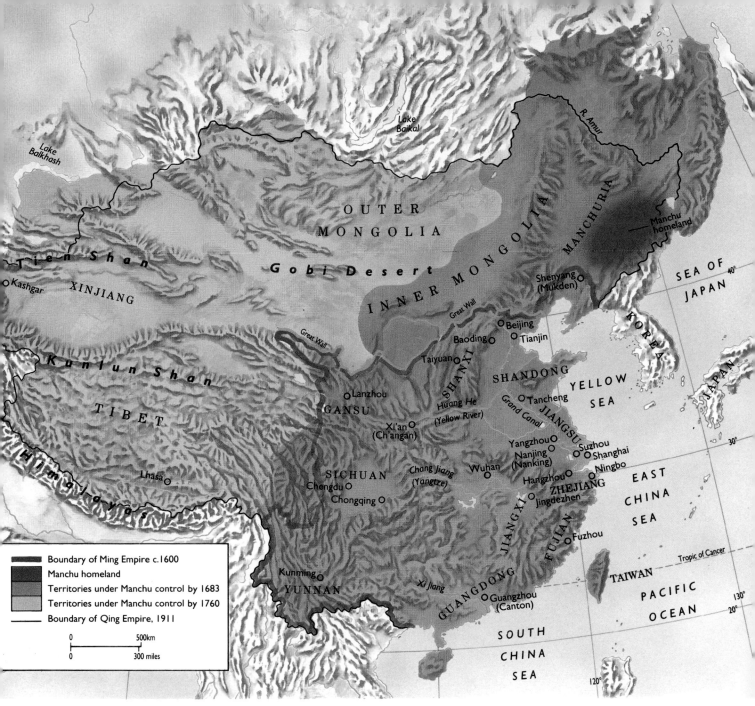

Lake Baikal

OUTER MONGOLIA

Gobi Desert

INNER MONGOLIA

MANCHURIA

Manchu homeland

R. Amur

SEA OF JAPAN

40°

Tien Shan

Kashgar

XINJIANG

Lake Balkhash

Shenyang (Mukden)

Great Wall

Baoding

Beijing

Tianjin

Taiyuan

SHANXI

SHANDONG

Tancheng

KOREA

JAPAN

YELLOW SEA

Kunlun Shan

TIBET

Lanzhou

GANSU

Huang He (Yellow River)

Great Wall

Xi'an (Ch'angan)

Grand Canal

JIANGSU

30°

Himalayas

Lhasa

SICHUAN

Chengdu

Chongqing

Chang Jiang (Yangtze)

Wuhan

Yangzhou

Nanjing (Nanking)

Suzhou

Shanghai

Ningbo

Hangzhou

ZHEJIANG

Jingdezhen

EAST CHINA SEA

JIANGXI

FUJIAN

Fuzhou

Kunming

YUNNAN

Xi Jiang

GUANGDONG

Guangzhou (Canton)

TAIWAN

Tropic of Cancer

PACIFIC OCEAN

130°

20°

SOUTH CHINA SEA

120°

Boundary of Ming Empire c.1600
Manchu homeland
Territories under Manchu control by 1683
Territories under Manchu control by 1760
Boundary of Qing Empire, 1911

0   500km
0   300 miles

QING REALMS The empire spread deep into central Asia from its core provinces along the coast and river valleys.

inland along the great basins of the Chang Jiang and Huang He (Yellow River).

Beijing had the advantage of being inside the Great Wall – the 2150 mile (3460 km) fortification originally built by the Qin emperors in the 3rd century BC – but near the empire's vulnerable northern frontier, adjoining regions in central Asia that were ripe for annexation.

Lacking manpower and experience, China's new conquerors had no option but to cooperate with the country's traditional ruling class of scholar-bureaucrats and the landowning gentry from which the

bureaucrats were mostly recruited. The Qing were, moreover, sincere admirers of Chinese culture and became enthusiastic devotees of its learning and lavish patrons of its arts.

This did not stop them from maintaining a dual identity as Manchu and adoptive Chinese. Their administrative procedures yoked Chinese officials with parallel Manchu or, sometimes, Mongol appointees. Routine reports in Chinese were shadowed by correspondence from Manchu informants – for the emperor's eyes only. Such devices meant that neither Chinese nor Manchus could gather too

much power into their hands. What did in the end limit the monarch's influence was the proliferation of officialdom and paperwork which had expanded fivefold by 1800. The Qing emperors became prisoners of their own highly sophisticated creation.

PEACE AND PROSPERITY

In the villages of China – where 90 per cent of the emperor's subjects lived – the change of dynasty made little difference. Under the Qing, as under the Ming, villages were administered by headmen and councils chosen using varying combinations of inheritance and co-option. Villagers were left to run their own affairs, providing they paid their taxes and supplied recruits for the army when required.

Most were content with this arrangement, knowing that the wisest course was to have as little as possible to do with officials and the law. Impartial in theory, the system of justice often proved arbitrary. Torture was routinely used to extract confessions. These often endorsed the conclusion a magistrate had come to independently of any evidence – or had been induced to reach by bribes.

After the Manchus had consolidated their conquest in the 1680s, China had more than a century of virtually uninterrupted peace and prosperity. In 1736 the treasury enjoyed a comfortable surplus, equal to about a third of the central government's entire annual income. By 1786 that surplus had trebled, enabling the regime to suspend taxes in

IMPERIAL PROGRESS
The Kangxi Emperor visits Jiangnan, the region south of the Chang Jiang (Yangtze) river, during a tour of his realms in 1699. Travel by water was usually smoother and safer and often faster than by land.

Europe and China began in the 16th century. The first detailed, accurate accounts of the 'Celestial Empire' began in 1584 in letters from the Jesuit missionary Matteo Ricci. A history, by another priest, Gonzalez de Mendoza, appeared the following year.

At that time, the curiosity flowed in both directions. The Kangxi Emperor – rulers were referred to in this way, using special 'reign' names assumed when they came to the throne – ruled from 1662 to 1722, and not only patronised Chinese learning but was also intrigued by things European. The Jesuits' technical skills earned them honoured places at court in such, often unlikely, roles as casters of cannon and calculators of calendars – they won few converts, by contrast, for the Catholic doctrines they were supposed to disseminate.

In the end, first-hand contact with China began to dampen Western enthusiasm. In 1793-4 Lord Macartney led a high-level mission from King George III to the long-lived Qianlong Emperor and was imperially snubbed for his pains. He summarised China in an appropriately maritime metaphor. At first glance, he said, it was like an imposing man-of-war but on closer inspection revealed itself to be a rotting hulk manned by an incompetent and cowardly crew.

continued on page 14

provinces stricken by harvest failures, to write off arrears and to fund hydraulic control schemes and costly campaigns of territorial expansion.

By the 1790s, however, the tide was turning. The court was having to draw on its own reserves to suppress a messianic insurrection led by the semi-secret White Lotus sect. This task took almost ten years, thanks to growing corruption which had diverted funds that were meant for the military budget.

A MODEL FOR MANKIND?

Early European visitors were impressed by the contrast between China and their own war-torn continent. Direct and continuing contact between

11

YIN AND YANG

Chinese thought regarded opposites as opposed –

but also intertwined and complementary.

THE MOST COMMON version of the Chinese creation myth held that the creator god Pangu was born from the egg of Chaos. His birth made the egg separate into heavy elements – *yin* – which formed the Earth and light ones – *yang* – which became the Heaven.

Yin and *yang* were fundamental to much Chinese thought. For the Chinese, opposites were always complementary aspects of a single whole, each side being in a sense embedded in the other. Thus they saw the material world as intertwined with, rather than separated from, the spiritual, non-material realm.

The notion of *yin* and *yang* carried this entwining of opposites into all the main areas of life. In traditional Chinese thought, *yang* represents all that is above, hot, light, hard, active and male. *Yin* stands for all that is below, cold, dark, soft, passive and female. *Yin* is present in even numbers, valleys and streams and is represented by the tiger, the colour orange and a broken line. *Yang* is present in odd numbers and mountains and it is represented by the dragon, the colour azure and an unbroken line.

Yin and *yang* apply in matters of health as well. In Chinese thought, the human – that is, inferior, material – soul (*po*) is distinguishable from a heavenly – superior, spiritual – counterpart (*hun*). Life and health flourish when the two are in harmony; divergence between them results in sickness and death. The earth-bound *po*, being *yin*, should be subservient to the ethereal *hun*, which is *yang*. Harmonious subordination can be disrupted by the passions to which the *po* is prey.

The bones of an ancestor and his grave, constitute a powerful repository of earthy *yin* forces, to be treated with respect. It is essential that the grave should be correctly located in the landscape. If not, the *po* may become a *gui* (malicious ghost) and, as a result, the beneficial influences of the dead person's *hun* may not be transmitted from the corpse to its descendants.

The philosopher Zou Yan, who died in the 3rd century BC, was an early exponent of the *yin-yang* system. He linked it with the theory that all aspects of nature consist of five 'elements' (*Wu Xing*) – metal,

MEANINGS WITHIN An 18th-century porcelain dish shows a shepherdess (*yin*) with three sheep, the symbol for which in Chinese script resembles the symbol for *yang*. Right: Fire (*yang*) combines with cloud (*yin*) to evolve as Vital Energy in a Taoist weather manual from the 19th century.

COMPELLING ATTRACTION The eyes of sage, scholar and infant are all drawn to the *yin-yang* symbol. The symbol – also shown in the carved pendant (below) – represents the interweaving nature of the two 'opposites'.

rest. Thus the year's four seasons proceeded from *yin*-in-*yin* (pure *yin*) – winter – through *yang*-in-*yin*, spring, to *yang*-in-*yang* (pure *yang*), summer, to *yin*-in-*yang*, autumn.

Yin-yang analysis was applied widely in medicine to classify organs, harmful influences and remedial therapies. A *yin* organ, such as the liver, subjected to excessive *yang* influences, such as heat, could be restored to balance by draining the heart to which it was known to supply *yang* influences, thus requiring it to part with its own excess of *yang*.

This would involve selecting an appropriate drug to penetrate the inner 'meridian' (or network) believed to link the liver and heart – both drug and network were also categorised in terms of *yin* and *yang*. Some medicinal compounds included 'guiding drugs' which were supposed to lead the way to the desired bodily meridian and the affected organ. This left the rest of the medicine to bring about the actual cure.

Yin-yang theory also underlay – and underlies – acupuncture. If the two forces are imbalanced, the result is a blockage in the flow of the vital life force (*ch'i*) which flows through the body's meridian networks – 12 of them in all. Acupuncture is believed to be a way of redistributing *yin* and *yang* through the meridians and thus restoring the flow of *ch'i* to harmony.

wood, fire, water and earth, whose changing combinations he believed to be governed by the interaction of *yin* and *yang*.

All essential categories of being – time, space, colour, number and ethical rules – could be classified as representative of either *yin* or *yang*. Furthermore, each always proceeded from its opposite, as night from day, high tide from ebb tide, male from female, movement from

PAYING TRIBUTE Kirghiz frontier nomads present prize mounts to the Qianlong Emperor in an 18th-century scroll.

By then decline was certainly in the air. After the death of the Qianlong Emperor in 1799, the line of able and energetic Qing rulers ended. The ill effects of corruption were compounded by unprecedented population pressure on the land, ruinous currency fluctuations, mass unemployment, banditry, natural disasters, famines and epidemics, opium addiction among all classes and the increasingly impudent incursions of well-armed and belligerent Western foreigners. These multiple afflictions provoked in turn a wave of massive and immensely destructive popular insurrections which may have cost 40 million lives or more over the course of the 19th century. They plunged the Celestial Empire into an inexorable downward spiral of misery.

In 1842 China was humiliatingly defeated at the hands of the British in the Opium War – a result of growing tensions between the Chinese authorities, anxious to put a stop to the British-controlled opium trade into their country, and their British counterparts, determined to continue the lucrative trade. After that, China was forced to open its frontiers to traders, to accept a Western military presence in certain 'treaty' ports and to

THE WESTERNERS' RELIGION Christian missionaries of around 1883 are surrounded by a group of their Chinese converts.

tolerate evangelisation by Christian missionaries. China's self-evident weakness completed the change in Western attitudes from admiration to contempt.

In vilifying China, Westerners gave themselves an excuse for its partition. Hong Kong was ceded to Britain in 1842. Russia took over the region north of the Amur river and western territories around the Ili river and Lake Balkhash; it also established a strategically invaluable, ice-free naval base at Port Arthur. Germany acquired Kiaochow and France Guangzhouwan. Japan astonished the world by routing Manchu forces in a six-month war in 1895, seizing Taiwan as a colony.

Faced with external aggression and internal disintegration, China's ruling class was divided in its response. A few sought 'self-strengthening' through importing Western technology and modernising the armed forces along Western lines. At different times and places this was spasmodically achieved. But the empire could not be saved by a few shipyards and arsenals and the vision of a handful of patriotic radicals. The court itself clung to past ways, once the key to imperial greatness. The Qing were thus conquered by their own conquest and secured their own extinction – and with it the catastrophic implosion of the world's largest society.

FAMILY LIFE IN IMPERIAL CHINA

In an uncertain world, where anarchy brought bandits and peace taxes
and where natural disaster could wipe out homes and harvests at any time,
a strong family network was the best cushion against catastrophe. In China this
network stretched far into the past and the future. Ancestors still lived in the
devotions of their descendants, and the living owed obligations not only to the dead
but also to those not yet born. To die childless was to render one's life worthless.

KITH AND KIN

The Chinese household was extended. If possible, the members of a family stayed together

under one roof, with common property, a shared income and shared obedience to one

family head. Children, even as adults, owed an absolute duty to their parents.

THE FAMILY was everything for the Chinese. Loyalty to the family was even more important than loyalty to the state, and it was a loyalty that carried over from generation to generation including dead forebears cared for through the rites of ancestor worship. Among the living, the ideal was a 'five-generation family' with great-grandparents, grandparents, parents, sons and the

sons' children building their home as as an ever-increasing unit.

In fact, very few families attained this goal, but it was certainly normal for eldest sons to bring their

ALL IN THEIR PLACES **A mandarin of the 1870s surveys the courtyard of his fine house, with his son standing beside him. The women and children watch from their own quarters upstairs.**

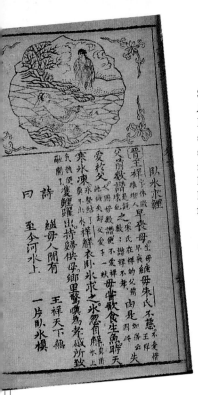

SHINING EXAMPLE
A 1688 edition of the Book of Filial Piety shows an exemplary son, Wang Xiang, melting river-ice with his body-heat so that his parents may eat fresh fish in winter.

wives into the family home and to live together with their parents. It was also quite common for other sons to follow their example, thus creating sizable three-generation families.

Large households like these with plenty of uncles, aunts, cousins and nephews as well as parents and grandparents were most common among better-off families, particularly in the fertile rice-growing south of China.

The family was a strictly hierarchical, in many ways very formal, world in which all relationships were conducted according to well-established codes of behaviour. Chinese society was based on an ancient tradition of 'Five Human Relationships': those between ruler and government minister, father and son, elder brother and younger brother,

husband and wife, friend and friend. All these relationships carried clear notions of superiority and subordination that reached into the heart of family life. Members of a family did not address each other by their names, for example, but rather by their position in the family hierarchy, using specific terms that meant 'younger brother' or 'father's younger brother's wife' and so on. There was no single word for brother, or even for aunt, uncle or cousin. If you wanted to say 'brothers', you had to say 'older brother and younger brother'.

In similar fashion, distinct attitudes were considered appropriate for each member of the family. Thus a father was supposed to show 'respect' for his children, while it was the mother's job to provide 'affection'. Wielding the firm hand of authority was the head of the family whose control over his sons and grandsons and their wives was virtually absolute and specifically encouraged by the state. The government's view was that obedience within the home instilled obedience to authority generally.

For children, meanwhile, encouragement in the practice of obedience came from the ancient, much-read text known as the *Xiaojing* ('Book of Filial Piety'), compiled by an unknown author some time before the 3rd century AD. Among the 24 'examples' it contained was the tale of Wu Meng, who allowed himself to be eaten by mosquitoes rather than brush them away in case they should

---

EYEWITNESS

THE SPIRIT OF SACRIFICE REAPS HEAVEN'S REWARD

EACH GENERATION passed on to the next the ideal of undying and unlimited respect for parents. In this example from the *Xiaojing* ('Book of Filial Piety'), veneration for one's mother is set above even love for a child:

❦ Guo Zhu was very poor. He had a son of three years. Every day Guo's mother kept back some of her own food so that her grandson

should not go hungry. Seeing this, Guo said to his wife: "We are too poor even to provide properly for our mother. We should get rid of our son. We can always have another son but never another mother."

A few days later Guo began to dig a grave. When he had dug down to waist-height he struck a buried vessel, filled with gold and

inscribed as follows: "Heaven sends this gold to Guo Zhu because he was ready to sacrifice his son for his mother's sake. This is the reward for his filial love. Let no official deprive him of it, and no other person dare to take it!"

Thus was the life of the child saved and the poor cottage made radiant by the splendour of miraculous gold. ❧

go on to attack his parents. Another fable told the story of Laizi who, when an adult, continued to dress as a child and play with toys to keep his parents happy.

THE THREE SUBORDINATIONS

The subordinate position of women was another notable feature of life. A woman's existence was known as one of three subordinations: first to her father; then on marriage to her husband; and finally to her eldest son when her husband died.

Women never ate with the male members of the household; they did not attend school; almost all jobs were closed to them. There were even limits on how much they could see of their own parents, brothers, sisters and other relatives after marriage. They could not own property; when they married their possessions went with them to the new home.

FAMILY DEFERENCE

Terms for family relationships were even used for acquaintances outside the family. So a younger man would address an older one as 'father's younger brother'; in the case of someone very old or greatly superior in rank, the younger man would call him 'father's elder brother'. Terms of respect for an elderly woman could be 'elder brother's wife' or 'father's elder sister'. As age was venerated in Imperial China, references to it were used to show deference.

Infant mortality rates were high and affected even the Imperial Family. The Kangxi Emperor, who reigned from 1662 to 1722, had 55 children, of whom 22 died before reaching the age of four. He and his two successors lost more than half their sons before the sons reached the age of 15.

Only in the most unusual circumstances did a bridegroom move into his wife's home, and that was generally because the wife's parents had no son of their own and the bridegroom had at least one brother to carry on his family line.

Continuity was the key to male dominance. The birth of a son was always a welcome event for parents because the son would carry on the family name and the family's inherited property. Even more importantly, he ensured continuity in the vital rituals of ancestor worship. A girl, by contrast, was no more than a temporary resident within the family. In time she would get married and move out

MOTHERS' JOY Women (above) play with infants on a sultry afternoon. A Hong Kong family (right) poses for the camera, the child on the right sitting astride a European hobbyhorse. Relationships between parents and children, husbands and wives were all regulated by ancient custom.

18

to her husband's household – hence the Chinese saying: 'A boy is born facing in, a girl facing out.'

Male heirs were so important that if a wife could not produce one, a man was perfectly entitled to take a concubine or concubines if he could afford the extra expense. Failing that, he might buy an unwanted male child from poor parents and adopt him. The roles of both concubines and adopted boys were acknowledged in law and accepted as normal.

For girls the prospects were quite different. Unwanted baby girls were sometimes 'exposed', drowned or buried alive at birth. Sir John Barrow, a member of the British embassy in 1793, reported that an average of 24 infants were left out to die each day in Beijing (Peking) – their bodies collected in carts at night. Some 50 years later a Chinese provincial governor wrote: 'I have heard of the prevalence of female infanticide in all parts of [the northern province of] Shaanxi. The first female birth may sometimes be salvaged with effort, but the subsequent births are usually drowned. There are even those who drown every female baby without keeping any . . . The poor regarded the practice as an almost legitimate means of maintaining their minimal standard of living and, in any case, as a dire economic necessity.'

Like boys, girls could be sold – in fact, this was commoner with girls who were sometimes sold as servants, concubines and prostitutes. A 19th-century British writer, Robert K. Douglas, recorded the prices obtained in Beijing: 'At the present day a young girl of ten or twelve is worth . . . from 30 to 50 *taels* [silver ounces] and young women commonly fetch from 250 to 300 *taels*. Poverty is the prime cause of the full markets; and especially in times of famine, drought and pestilence, it is

common for men who at other times would shrink with abhorrence from the deed, to sell their wives and daughters to the highest bidders . . . [In] all large towns there are recognised brokers who deal in these human wares.'

LIVING THE FOUR VIRTUES

Despite such hazards, the vast majority of girls did, of course, survive babyhood. They learnt as early as possible the duties of baby-minding, household chores and the codes of behaviour that were expected of women, notably the four virtues of fidelity, cautious speech, industriousness and graceful manners.

They were being trained for marriage, the great event in every girl's life, though the choice of partner was not one in which she – or for that matter the bridegroom – played any part. Nor did she have any choice in the timing. Both sons and daughters married in order of birth, eldest first.

Finding the spouse was the parents' job, and they went about it with care, each family making inquiries into the financial

LOOK AND LEARN A woman spinner stares at the camera, with her child at her side. Children habitually saw their parents at work and so acquired their skills as a matter of course.

affairs of the other and the astrological compatibility of the pair as well as weighing up considerations such as 'class'. Not surprisingly, it was most normal for partners to be selected from within the same social grouping in accordance with the Chinese proverb: 'Wooden gates match with wooden gates and bamboo doors with bamboo doors.'

Since the bride and groom were unknown to each other before their wedding day, it did not really matter at what age a betrothal was arranged. It usually took place when the girl was around 11 years old.

These arrangements were always made through go-betweens who conducted all the negotiations,

including agreeing the size of the bride's dowry and fixing the wedding day. Another Chinese proverb says: 'Without clouds in the sky there is no rain. Without go-betweens there is no marriage.' The intermediaries were professionals, sometimes men but also often women who thus pursued one of the few jobs open to them.

Their activities were performed according to the 'Six Rites'. These began when the boy's family offered a gift to the girl's – if it was accepted, it meant that the proposal was being taken seriously. Then came the exchange of 'Eight Characters' defining the year, month, date and hour of birth of both the boy and the girl (this was important for

WEDDING MARCH The passage of a bridal chair – closed for modesty – is accompanied by an immodest din from flutes, gongs and fireworks.

astrological reasons). After that came the ritual vetting of the Eight Characters by a professional fortuneteller or astrologer. Then came the payment of a 'bride price' to the girl's family which, if accepted, amounted to formal betrothal. Next the date of the wedding was fixed. Last of all came the arrival of the bride at her new family home and the marriage ceremonial itself.

Only when the date of the wedding had been fixed was the bride informed of her impending

TEENAGE NUPTIALS A youthful bride and groom photographed in Shanghai in the 1870s face the future together, each arrayed in silk and satin finery. Brides might be as young as 15 when they married.

it is her parents who decide on it – and she has been kept in utter ignorance of it. Now, when the time to be married out of her home is near at hand, she may be deceived no longer, and it is only when she is formally acquainted with the fact that she becomes aware that she is about to be married out as someone's wife. From the moment of her telling onwards, her freedom of movement is limited and her rising and living, drinking and eating, sitting, sleeping and working all are confined to one place (usually upstairs in the house).'

After Knowing the Day, came the great day when the bridegroom sent a red bridal chair to the girl's family home – red was regarded as an auspicious and joyful colour. The girl did not touch the ground from the time she left her old home to the moment of her arrival at the new one. This practice, believed to protect her from evil spirits, was so deep-rooted that it continued after the Imperial age under the People's Republic – except that the brides rode bicycles.

At the bridegroom's home, groom and bride paid homage to Heaven and Earth and performed a

marriage. Traditionally this happened 30 days beforehand. A Chinese account, from the southeast of the country, describes the procedures: 'One month before she leaves her natal home, the bride's family go through the ceremony called "Knowing the Day". This is because her wedding is something completely outside the bride's control –

SEALING THE ALLIANCE A 19th-century painting shows a marriage ceremony. Marriage meant the linking not just of the bride and groom but also of two family networks.

**DISORDERLY CONDUCT
A Western account of
Chinese life shows a
prostitute being punished
by a mandarin's official.**

ceremony in honour of his
ancestors. At that point the
marriage was made, though
full completion waited until
after the feast when, accompanied by the relatives of the
groom, they went for the
ordeal known as the 'Distur-
bance of the Room'. Thus,
the consummation of the
marriage was appropriately a
family affair, though one for the groom's family
only. The bride's parents were not even present – it
was, on the other hand, customary for the newly
married couple to spend a few days with the bride's
parents after the wedding.

A LIFE OF INEQUALITIES

Inequalities continued in the new world the wife
had entered. It was socially unacceptable for a man
to be seen outside his home in the company of
women. So both his dinner parties at home and
visits to restaurants or theatres in town were all-male

affairs. Visiting the riverside city of Tongzhou, Sir
John Barrow was enchanted to find that 'the plain
between the landing-place and the temple
was like a fair, and cakes, rice, tea and
fruit upon masses of ice, and many
other refreshments were exposed for
sale, under large square umbrellas that
served instead of booths'. But, he added,
not 'a single woman appeared among the
many thousand spectators that were
assembled on the plain'. China was a seg-
regated society.

It was almost unheard of for a wife to
abandon a husband, and severe punishments were laid down if she did. Under the
Qing legal code, a wife could legally leave
her husband only if he mutilated or wounded
her severely or made her commit sexual acts with
others. Otherwise, a runaway wife was classified as
an unlawful fugitive and liable to 100 strokes of the
cane, as was anyone who helped or sheltered her.

However, a husband could divorce his wife
under what were called the 'Seven Outs': barrenness; infidelity; neglecting her parents-in-law;

**OCCASIONAL INDULGENCE Dalliance with a
courtesan, such as this one photographed in the
1870s, was permitted to prosperous married
men – provided they never took the relationship
seriously enough to threaten family or business.**

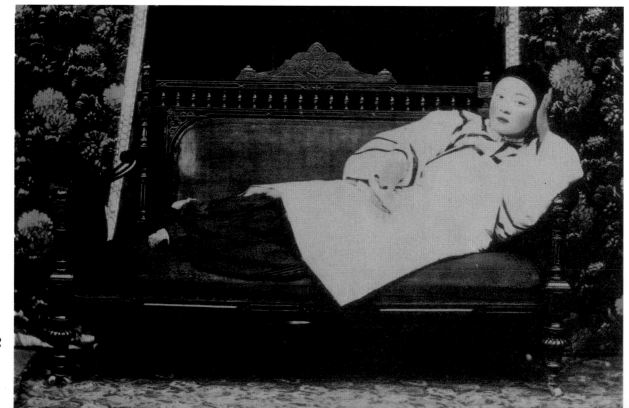

THE DELIGHTS OF A LILY FOOT

AROUND THE AGE of four or five, Chinese girls started on the agonising business of foot-binding. This created a hoof-shaped 'lily foot', depriving women of the ability to walk without support. For men, the 'lily foot' exercised a strong erotic appeal, acknowledged even by those who in the later years of the empire favoured abolishing the custom. Foot-binding had the additional advantage, from the male point of view, of effectively disabling women and confining them to the home, thus reducing the chances of infidelity.

It was a painful process. Girls who underwent it later than early childhood had their bones broken and compressed. The feet were easily infected because the bindings were never changed until they fell to pieces. Mary Bryson, a British missionary writing in the 1880s, gave a description of the technique: 'One end of the strip of cotton is placed beneath the instep, and then carried over the four small toes, drawing them down beneath the foot. Another twist draws the heel and great toe nearer together, making an indentation beneath the sole. When all the cloth has been used, the end is firmly sewed down, and the feet are left for a week or two . . . Clean bandages are now and then put on, but the change has to be very rapidly effected, or the blood begins again to circulate in the poor benumbed feet, and the agony becomes almost unbearable. Not unfrequently during the process a girl loses one or two of her toes; but she feels repaid for the pain she endures by being the possessor of still smaller feet.'

In China, foot-binding had social distinction, for the poorest families could not afford to have their daughters immobilised when their help was needed around the home. Foot-binding was one custom the formerly nomadic Manchus never adopted. Even so, there were many Manchu girls who envied the mincing 'lily walk' of their Chinese counterparts.

TREADING LIGHTLY The swaying saunter of a fashionable Chinese woman with bound feet was the visual equivalent of a delicate tune.

---

garrulousness; theft; jealousy and bad temper; and incurable disease. Her protection was confined to 'Three Not-Outs' which saved her if she had mourned correctly for either of her parents-in-law, if her husband's family had become wealthy after marriage, or if she had no home to go back to. The fear of barrenness was one reason why concubines, whose arrival was also organised by go-betweens, were often welcomed by the wife.

Concubines had a well-established role in family life, though wives always took precedence over them. To establish her inferior status a concubine was often obliged to perform a ritual when introduced into a family: for example, she would make tea for the wife and present it to her. The concubine's children were regarded as legitimate, though they did not inherit equally with the wife's and her punishments were heavier than a wife's would be if she committed any crimes against the husband. A husband's offences against his concubine were dealt with more leniently than any he might commit against his wife and sometimes a concubine would be excluded from the various ancestral rites performed in the home. Nevertheless, concubines were regarded as a husband's natural entitlement, and Chinese society did not frown on prostitution either.

Despite the husband's near-absolute rights over his wife, her first crucial relationship was not so much with him as with her mother-in-law. Chinese novels frequently describe the animosities between them and the indignities inflicted on the young wife, for it was the mother-in-law's job to begin the next phase of the bride's training, teaching her such all-important tasks as how to prepare the right food for her husband.

One way of eliminating such tensions was for families to adopt a prospective daughter-in-law and bring her up as a member of their own household. Then, when the time came for marriage, she was already fully trained and had learned to regard her mother-in-law as a mother. Nevertheless, in most families where the tensions did exist, they lasted until the wife gave birth to an heir which gave her a status and position of her own.

Within the household the father was a remote figure. A Chinese writer, Martin C. Yang, described

the traditional patterns of life in a village in Shandong province: 'The relationship between father and child has none of the warmth and freedom existing between mother and child. The father's attitude is dignified, even remote; his authority is unquestioned and he expects submissiveness from his sons . . . When the son is an infant, the father may on rare occasions play with him or take him out. When the boy is old enough to help in the fields, father and son walk together and work together quite often.'

Things changed when the boy reached the age of about 15, however. At this point, 'the father assumes a more dignified attitude towards [his son] and is frequently severe. The son feels uncomfortable with his father and prefers to work with other men in the fields. When father and son do work together, they have nothing to say, and even at home they speak only when there is business to discuss. At street gatherings or in places of amusement they mutually avoid each other.'

From the age of nine or ten, boys were entirely separated from their sisters, thus encouraging the

No, No, Do it Again! In a prosperous house with many servants the daughter-in-law might be spared much heavy work, but she still had to display refined domestic accomplishments to the standard expected by her mother-in-law.

'cold and ceremonious conduct' that Sir John Barrow noticed between family members. Barrow found it distressing that the 'little incidents and adventures of the day', accounts of which enlivened 'many a long winter's evening by a comfortable fireside, in our own country, are in China buried in silence'. He also noted that 'the young people have no occasional meetings for the purpose of dancing and of exercising themselves in feats of activity'.

CHILDHOOD REGIMES
Chinese children had, in fact, little of what we would think of as a childhood. At first, it is true, they were indulged. As babies and infants they were constantly in the arms of, or on the back of, an adult – either the mother who would breast-feed at the slightest sign of unhappiness, or perhaps a

doting grandfather. At this stage, Chinese parents were rarely over-fussy about toilet training or tantrums. But the indulgences of infancy ended suddenly about the age of five or six when boys began their work in the fields, or went to school, and girls were introduced to the foot bandages that would eventually cripple them. Formality took over and discipline became the rule. Beatings of boys and girls by fathers and mothers were universal and frequent. It was not long before a Chinese youth had learned to behave with adult gravity.

Only relatively prosperous families could spare their sons from working the family fields and send

them to school. The boy offered this opportunity found a monotonous, regulated regime. The best teachers were employed privately by families who could afford them; those in village schools were often failed candidates for the entrance examinations of the imperial civil service and sometimes they were scarcely literate. The schools were dirty, one-roomed and dark. Teachers did not 'teach' in the Western sense but saw their job as keeping order and handing out assignments.

Arriving every morning at dawn, the children brought their own benches and tables, together with brushes and inks for calligraphy. They were not separated into classes, so ages in the schoolroom ranged from five to twenty. They began the day memorising their texts – the classical writings attributed to Confucius and his followers – by constant repetition. When the teacher entered, each boy chanted what he had learned and received his next assignment. After that boys and teacher went home to breakfast. Back at the schoolhouse following breakfast, the pupils spent the rest of the morning practising calligraphy and perhaps drawing. After lunch came the same patterns of rote learning until dusk. There was no physical education: the body was too precious to risk playing games.

Yet if childhood had its drawbacks, at least the birth of a boy was a matter for family rejoicing. Thirty days after the birth came the

DIVINE PRESENCE A scroll, table, candles, incense and offerings of food constitute a domestic shrine. It was a constant reminder of the household gods believed to guard each family from ill-fortune.

25

Full Month Feast when the boy was given the first of the many names he would acquire during his lifetime. This was his 'milk name', sometimes chosen deliberately in order to mislead any malevolent spirits. Thus he might be called 'dog' or 'chicken' – evil spirits were not considered likely to

be interested in lower forms of life – or by a girl's name. Later a boy had a 'book name' given by his teacher when he started school, a 'style name' for family use when he married, a 'pen name' if he wrote, an 'official name' for his rank and a 'posthumous name' for use by posterity. A style name might, say, be Liu Baonan, 'Treasure of the South'; an official name, Chuzhen, 'Pillar of the State of Chu'. The posthumous name might incorporate some code known to the family circle, giving the deceased person's exact position in the family hierarchy.

CONCENTRATE! Good calligraphy required an upright posture, a steady wrist and flexible fingers. Schools like this one trained all their pupils to write right-handed.

The Chinese were also very fond of nicknames – a woman's nickname, in particular, was often her only claim to individuality, since she was rarely known as anything other than her husband's wife or her son's mother. Girls' milk names tended to be taken from the virtues it was hoped they would develop: Jade for beauty, Chastity, Thrift. Often girls' names were given without a Full Month Feast or any event to mark the occasion, and the use of the name did not normally last beyond childhood. An adult woman was commonly known by her husband's surname plus a word signifying that she was female: 'Woman' Peng, for example.

The birth of a boy was important, but after that individual birthdays were rarely celebrated. It is true that the exact hour, day, month and year of a birth were recorded in the form of the Eight

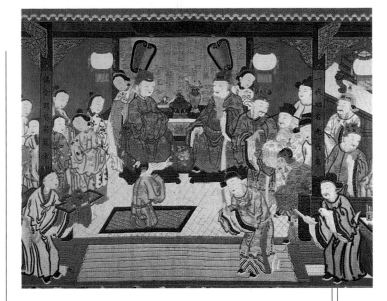

A BIG DAY A boy's coming of age was marked by religious ceremonies and feasting. This depiction comes from an 18th-century embroidered hanging.

A VILLAGE SCHOOL TEACHER

HE XIAN drew his threadbare robe still tighter around his thin shoulders, crouched even closer to the tiny charcoal brazier at his feet and determined not to think about the cold. The one-room schoolhouse next to the temple compound was no more than a leaky shack. His own home was scarcely better. How ill-timed that wretched fever had been – wrecking his chances in the county examination, the first rung on the ladder to mandarin status. His family simply could not afford to support him for another year. So he had left home to support himself as a teacher until such time as his fortunes allowed him another attempt. It was little comfort to him that he was rather a good teacher – which meant that, despite his feeble frame, he was quite willing and able to thrash any boy who dared to distract any other. Most of his pupils

were in awe of his literacy and invariably cowed by his favourite sarcasm – 'This is not a Tatar tavern!' – snarled if the noise level in the room irritated him.

Mr He was less a teacher in the active sense than a mentor, examiner and disciplinarian. Simply by being literate and having the manners of a gentleman, he was a model of what the brightest and most determined village boys might aspire to. Because his pupils varied in age from five to nearly twenty it was impossible to instruct them as a group. Each boy worked at his own pace, depending on his ability and the number of days his father could spare him from the fields. The youngest concentrated on mastering the basic written characters made using three or four strokes of the calligraphy brush, the oldest on memorising passages from classic

writings attributed to Confucius and his followers. Each came up to Mr He when summoned to show his work or recite his assignment. There was one pupil, he thought, who had the makings of a scholar.

After the last lad had been dealt with Mr He glanced up and barked 'Go!' The room emptied rapidly. Mr He trudged to his lodgings and contemplated his lunch with disgust. To be reduced to eating millet porridge, like the lowest peasant!

The afternoon class was much smaller, as he had anticipated, leaving him more time to concentrate on his star pupil. If only he would make even faster progress. Mr He could go to his father, a merchant of modest fortune and immodest ambition, and suggest extra sessions of private tutoring. It was his best hope of extra cash and an end to this dismal humiliation.

Characters later exchanged as part of the ritual of betrothal, but this was important for astrological reasons only. The one exception to this rule was the head of the family whose immense authority increased still further with age. Elaborate festivities were common when he reached a significant age such as 60, when presents symbolising longevity were offered to him. These might include plates of peaches (a fruit associated with long life) – the peaches were either real or painted onto porcelain.

For the rest, the real birthday to enjoy was the New Year when everybody became a year older. This was – and still is – the greatest and most colourful of all Chinese celebrations, with street processions, music, lanterns, carnival dragons and

HIS PEOPLE'S FATHER Crowds gather to see the Kangxi Emperor. Duty to parents was believed to encourage duty to the emperor and state. In Confucius' words: 'Few indeed are those who are naturally filial towards their parents . . . but are fond of opposing their superiors . . .'

fireworks. It was a seven-day event with each of the first six days representing the animals and crops necessary for human survival. The first day was the birthday of chickens, the second of dogs; then came pigs, ducks, oxen and horses, while the seventh day was celebrated as the universal birthday of humankind. The horse's birthday was auspicious for visiting relatives, but on the seventh day the tradition was to stay at home and eat red beans – seven for men and fourteen for women. Beans, as seeds, signified children, fertility, the all-important continuation of the family line.

THE POWER OF A LINEAGE

Just as heads of families had legal backing for exercising powerful control in the home, so too did the heads of wider groups of families known as lineages. A lineage was a number of related families which often comprised the population of a particular village

RETURN TO CHILDHOOD Grandfather and grandson together enjoy the performance of a street-corner puppeteer. Traditional pastimes united different generations because they shared a common culture.

TELL ME AGAIN Wealthy families could afford private tutors for their sons. The exam-based meritocracy was always skewed in favour of families who were already successful.

and whose numbers could vary from hundreds to, occasionally, thousands. Lineages owned their own property, had their own incomes and some became very rich. Their origins lay in the splitting of a family's property equally among sons. Often part of the property was set aside for aged parents and subsequently this was held collectively in trust by the sons and their descendants. With each generation and each split, the property held in trust would probably be added to, so that the income eventually derived from it could be considerable.

Lineages were governed by a Council of Elders, almost always males over the age of 65. If the lineage was rich, the Council might use its money to organise the acquisition of more property, provide irrigation, dams, bridges, schools or

THE LAW IS NOT MOCKED

THE QING legal code, wishing to encourage widows to honour the memories of their husbands, decreed that the property she inherited from him, plus her original dowry, should pass back to his family if she remarried. Unfortunately this high-minded ruling often had an unintended negative effect because it gave a man's family a clear incentive to pressure his widow into remarriage against her will. In this way the family rid themselves of the cost of supporting her and her children and made a profit at the same time.

In 1670 Woman Peng, in the city of Tancheng in Shandong province, found herself in just such a situation, harassed by the three Chen brothers who were great-nephews of her late husband. When she stubbornly resisted them they looked for another way to get her land and so decided to kill her schoolboy son, Lian, instead. In the absence of a direct male heir, Woman Peng's property would revert to them anyway.

The problem then facing the Chens was how to kill Lian and to incur only a minimal penalty from the courts. One of the Chens knew enough law to see a possible course of action by invoking the legal right of vengeance. The Chens' father had been killed in the coup of 1643 that brought the Qing dynasty to power, although exactly how, where and by whom no one knew, since the corpse itself had never been recovered. Why not blame Lian's dead father? Chen Guoxiang could then avenge his father's spirit by killing Lian, mitigating his action by claiming it to be an act of filial piety. For additional security he would carry out the dreadful deed while in a (feigned) state of intoxication.

On July 6, 1670, Chen Guoxiang walked to Lian's school, carrying with him the sort of sturdy wooden paddle used to beat washing. When the children told him that their teacher was absent, Chen grabbed Lian, dragged him outside and, in front of the temple of the Goddess of Mercy and the boy's terrified school-fellows, battered him to death.

The next morning Chen gave himself up to the magistrates, admitting the murder but claiming that he had bumped into Lian by accident and therefore had acted without premeditation, that he had only been doing his filial duty and that anyway he had been drunk at the time.

The magistrates were less than impressed with this confused line of defence. Lian's schoolmates readily testified that Chen had come to their classroom on purpose, armed with the paddle and sober. Under cross-examination the Chen brothers then directly contradicted each other over exactly where Lian's father was supposed to have murdered their father. Nor could they produce a single witness who had ever heard them pledge to seek out and revenge themselves upon his killer. Indeed, all the evidence demonstrated that they had lived in complete harmony with the alleged killer for almost 30 years.

The examining magistrate observed dryly that Lian's father had indeed been a singularly lucky man not to have met one of the Chens in a drunken frenzy even once in all that time. Chen Guoxiang's attempt to claim the protection of the law for an act of filial piety was therefore dismissed out of hand. He was instead condemned for the deliberate murder of a close relative and sentenced to death by the appropriate method – strangulation.

---

perhaps endowments to enable students to study for government exams. In other words, a Council acted as a provider of local government and welfare. Even more importantly, it organised worship for the lineage's common ancestors at an Ancestral Hall.

Lineages were essential to Chinese society, officially responsible for enforcing many aspects of the law and for collecting taxes. Their role differed from place to place. In one case lineage leaders were required to 'administer corporal punishment at the ancestral hall to a member who commits an illegal offence which is punishable under the law by flogging. However, if it is a criminal offence subject to penal servitude, the guilty member shall be sent to the government.' Another lineage was allowed to pass the death sentence 'so as to avoid legal trial which brings shame on the ancestors'.

A reverse process also operated whereby offences committed by an individual could bring state punishment upon the whole family. In the case of a capital crime, the Qing legal code laid it down that the criminal's parents, brothers and sisters, wife and children should all be executed with him. For lesser crimes, the offender's family members were enslaved.

CITY PLEASURES

Evening is drawing in and an audience gathers on a piece of open ground in a Chinese city. They are there to watch a troupe of actors perform to strident musical accompaniment. Further entertainment comes from a tightrope walker displaying his skills nearby.

Popular drama owed little to the educated classes. Produced by actors for a restless and untutored clientele, it relied on eye-catching costumes, extravagant gestures, improbable plots and the stylised characterisation of heroes, heroines, gods, demons, warriors and clowns. Make-up usually confirmed each character's nature and role. Actions were underlined by symbolic props such as lanterns, whips, oars or swords.

Many actors were also accomplished acrobats and jugglers. Their talents may have drawn audiences but did little to draw respect. As constant travellers, acting troupes were regarded by the authorities as little better than vagabonds.

ANCESTOR WORSHIP

The Chinese family reached both backwards and forwards in time. At the heart

of home and family life was the household shrine where the living paid their dues

to the dead and hoped themselves to receive theirs in turn one day.

EVERY Chinese home had a household shrine where the family burnt incense and made offerings to its ancestors. These shrines were not tucked away – on the contrary, they were placed prominently, often in the main hall. The ancestors' spirits were thus ever-present, keeping an eye on what was going on. They were a constant reminder that family life stretched beyond the grave and that watchful ancestors continued to be involved in the affairs of the living. Important business, such as the betrothal of a son or daughter, or the purchase of extra land, was invariably reported to the ancestors in prayers asking them to bring success.

Ancestor worship went to the heart of Chinese life, affecting relationships inside and outside the family, everyday behaviour and the structure of society itself. For example, when parents worshipped at the shrines of their own deceased parents, they were setting an example for their children – an example of the respect they expected from their children while they were still alive, as well as the continued reverence they expected after their deaths. It followed, too, that a person must respect himself – for he was destined in time to be worshipped. Continuity was all-important for the Chinese, with everything seen as an inheritance from the past and a legacy for the future. Out of reverence for his forebears and for the sake of posterity, the individual had both to behave properly and to take care of his body.

According to the *Xiaojing*, the much-revered ancient text on filial duty: 'It is the first principle of filial piety that you dare not injure your body, limbs, hair or skin, which you received from your father and mother.' Such precepts gave the Chinese a particular horror of losing parts of their body – beyond the fear of pain or inconvenience that anyone would feel. For this reason, beheading was a more severe punishment for criminals than

DAILY DUTY Women bring offerings of tea and fruit to a family shrine. For most Chinese their ancestors were a more real presence than the spirits of heaven-dwelling deities.

WORDS OF WISDOM Behind the women and children of a family from Sichuan (above) is the family shrine with moral texts hung up at the back. Geomancers, using compasses like this (right), ensured the 'lucky' siting of homes and graves, important for family prosperity.

15th days of each lunar month, corresponding to the full and new moons, when more elaborate offerings were made. Then, in addition to tea and incense, food and money were also left at the shrines. Even more special were the ceremonies observed on days such as the ancestors' birth dates, death dates, and above all at the Chinese New Year – a movable feast, like the Christian Easter, which usually falls in late January or early February. The ancestors were also part of family celebrations such as a Full Month Feast, when a baby was 30 days old, or a family wedding.

hanging (unlike Western practice where beheading was reserved for the well-born). In China, victims paid their executioners to sew their heads back on after their deaths.

A household shrine had the names of the family's ancestors displayed on wooden boards or tablets. A perpetual light – made from a wick placed in a bowl of oil – burned before it, while incense and offerings of tea were presented every day. As likely as not it was the women of the family who performed these day-to-day rituals, but on special occasions – and there were many of them – the men took the lead. Such occasions punctuated family life and included celebrations on the 1st and

The ancestors were meant to earn their keep. The more lavish the worship accorded them, the more benevolent they were supposed to become and the more active in the interests of the living. The Chinese believed that the afterlife resembled the world they knew and that their ancestors had a power and status that reflected their influence while on Earth. So achievements like obtaining an important job or passing one of the government examinations not only reflected credit on the individual and his living relatives, but also gave the successful person a status that was carried on after his death. For that reason ancestors' tablets sometimes recorded the dates of significant successes as well as their names and birth and death dates.

DEGREES OF MOURNING

In these circumstances, it is not surprising that the rituals of death, laid down in great detail by both law and custom, had profound significance for the Chinese. For children, mourning was sacrosanct. The most powerful of government ministers had to

resign his job and go home when his father died. Failure to do so was punishable by instant dismissal, flogging and sometimes banishment.

Principles of filial piety had huge ramifications. In Chinese society all relationships were based on superiority and inferiority. The young revered the old and the female revered the male, but the duties of children to their parents took precedence over all. This affected manners, morals, customs and the law. The penalty for a son who struck his father was decapitation – while there was no punishment for a father who beat his son mercilessly.

FOND FAREWELL A family mourns its dead father. A priest chants, and relatives support the chief mourner, the eldest son. Laid out on the table beside the dead man are his best clothes.

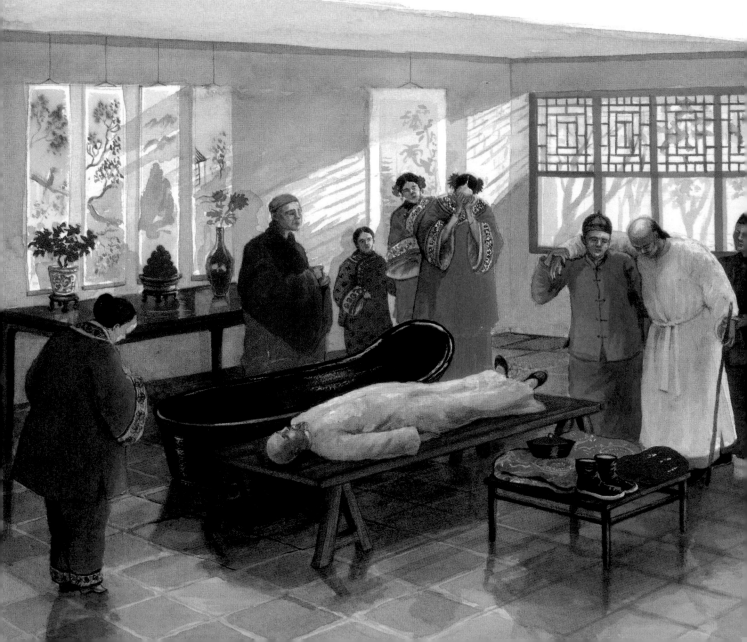

The intricate web of family ties was regulated by state laws based on the degrees of kinship known collectively as the *wufu*. The phrase means 'the five kinds of clothing' and relates to the various types of mourning dress worn for prescribed periods by each member of a family.

The first degree of mourning and its dress were the prerogative of children on the death of either of their parents. It lasted 27 months, during which time the mourner wore coarse unhemmed clothing, a hemp headdress, grass sandals, and carried a mourning staff. The second grade included people who had lost a spouse, child or grandparent. They wore coarse hemmed garments, straw or hemp shoes, but otherwise dressed as those in grade one. The mourning period varied from three months to one year according to the degree of kinship.

Mourning in the third degree lasted nine months and embraced those whose unmarried daughters, brothers, sisters or grandchildren had died. They wore coarse cloth. The fourth degree wore less coarse cloth for a period of five months and included people mourning the death of a sister-in-law or a great-uncle. The fifth-grade mourners – those mourning, for example, remote cousins – were allowed dresses of plain silk which they wore for three months.

The *wufu* was supposed to cover all possible relationships within the ideal five generations of a family unit. Underlining the fact that the relationship between the living and the dead was a matter of male descent, the full network applied only to the male side. The duties of a wife towards her own original family were less extensive and on her mother's side applied only to her mother, her maternal grandparents, uncles, aunts, nephews and male first cousins.

THE ETIQUETTE OF BEREAVEMENT

Mourning was, in effect, the first stage in ancestor worship. Theoretically, this could continue down the male line of a family for ever. In practice, of course, it did not. For one thing there was not

PATERNAL PROTECTION The portrait of a father or ancestor might be worn as an amulet to ward off ill-fortune.

enough room for an indefinite number of tablets to be displayed in the household shrine. So, with exceptions for the tablets of founding and other distinguished ancestors, they were periodically weeded out. Those removed were either buried or taken to the ancestral hall of the family's lineage.

This was the last stage of a process that had begun generations before. Every time a parent died, it triggered a sequence that was performed in similar circumstances in households all over the empire. The rituals began before death when, for example, an elderly father was clearly seen to be dying.

The old man was taken to the central hall of the house and laid on a bed of boards with his feet pointing to the door. His best clothes were placed by his side. When he died, a Buddhist priest was summoned to chant over the body – the rites of death tended to be monopolised by Buddhism which had the best-defined beliefs about the afterlife. Meanwhile, relatives helped to prop up the chief mourner – generally the eldest son – who was supposed to be too grief-stricken to be able to stand or walk unaided; he also had a special mourning staff. According to custom the son went to the nearest stream or river to 'buy water' for a ritual cleansing of the corpse.

The quality of the coffin was laid down by law and varied according to the social status of the family. In all cases, it was likely to be massive – made of the hardest, best-quality wood affordable,

COMPARATIVE POPULATIONS

In 1800 China had a population of more than 300 million, making it ten times as populous as its neighbour, Japan. Britain's population was on a par with Spain, just over 10 million. The United States was on a par with Ireland, at just over 5 million.

REST IN PEACE? AT A PRICE

FOR THE CHINESE important rituals had to coincide with favourable cosmic forces. This sometimes left them vulnerable to unscrupulous pressure, as the American missionary, the Rev Justus Doolittle, observed in the 1850s:

❝ When burials connected with wealthy families take place . . . beggars often interfere for the purpose of getting food or money . . . According to the superstitious views of the Chinese, the burial should take place at a time fixed by the fortunetellers in order to be propitious, and the beggars take advantage of this fact to hinder and harass, in the hope of getting more money to keep quiet.

On the occasion of the burial of a native Christian . . . a company of beggars and lepers gathered around the grave and demanded 20 000 cash [copper coins] as the condition of allowing the coffin to be lowered . . . One of the rabble actually got down into the grave and . . . prevented the lowering of the coffin. The burial was delayed . . . until near dark, when, finding, contrary to usual custom, that no hour was fixed for the consummation of the burial . . . they were glad to accept 800 cash. ❞

3-4 in (7.5-10 cm) thick. The body in it rested on a coating of quicklime and charcoal and items such as coins and perhaps books were added before the coffin was closed and sealed. The coffin then remained unburied for 49 days, the traditional period of judgment in Buddhism, after which the soul was free to go to Heaven.

Ritual weeping by the various family members, which had started at the moment of death, continued during the 49 days of mourning. For the unwary it could be something of a pitfall, since anyone who did not express his or her grief satisfactorily was showing disloyalty to both the dead and the family group – a charge frequently levelled

LAST JOURNEY Professional mourners carry banners, umbrellas and other usual accessories of a funeral. One scatters white paper circles into the air, believed to help the soul to find its way back home. The chief mourner has his head bowed and carries a crook-like mourning staff.

at a bride newly married into the family. She might very well have little to weep about – after all the deceased might be her tyrannical mother-in-law – but correct behaviour was nonetheless expected.

When the coffin was finally removed to the grave-side, families organised the longest and most elaborate ceremony they could afford – often, indeed, more expensive than they could properly afford. Professionals were hired for the procession, a man with a long streamer of white cloth, the 'soul cloth', leading the way. He was followed by others carrying banners, one holding a white cock to summon the soul to accompany its body. Others carried a sedan chair for the ancestral tablet. In front of the coffin the eldest son and male mourners marched in strict order of precedence; females followed behind the coffin. The mourners wept loudly, led by a professional weeper who knew the correct degrees of grief expected from wives, sons, concubines, daughters, brothers and so on.

After the burial, the mourners returned to the home in the same order as for the procession to the grave. They then celebrated 'the feast of the dead' during which they placed the ancestral tablet in position on the household altar. The transition from earthly respects to ancestor worship had been made.

Bribes in the Afterlife

Ancestors had needs similar to those of the living – home, clothes, money and food. Apart from food, all these could be supplied as paper models which were carried in the funeral procession and then burnt at the graveside. Shops sold paper houses, clothes, furniture, horses, servants, sedan chairs, plates, swords – everything possible to equip the

---

PUNISHMENTS TO FIT THE CRIME

Under the Manchu legal code assaults were punished on a scale that allocated a set number of blows with the cane according to the severity of any injury caused:

Striking with hand or foot but not causing injury: 20 blows

Striking with hand or foot and causing injury: 30 blows

Striking with an object but causing no injury: 30 blows

Striking with an object and causing injury: 40 blows

Tearing out more than one inch of hair: 50 blows

Causing internal bleeding: 80 blows

Throwing excrement at another person's head: 80 blows

Breaking a tooth or bone or injuring an eye: 100 blows

In cases of permanent injury the guilty party forfeited half his property, which was used to support the injured person.

---

soul for its afterlife, including paper money to bribe spirit-world officials just as living ones were bribed in this world.

Food offered at the shrine, however, was real and was left just long enough for the ancestors to enjoy the 'essence' of it. Then it was removed for the household meal. The ancestors were given a meal cooked and prepared as if they were still members of the household. It included perhaps an ancestor's favourite dishes accompanied by the inevitable cooked rice and, of course, chopsticks. Regular food offerings continued to be made long after the funeral at festivals such as the New Year.

These offerings all reflected widely held beliefs about spirits. For the Chinese, a dead person had three souls. One went to the spirit world; one remained at the grave, and one existed with the tablet at the shrine. The soul bound for the spirit world had an awesome task ahead of it. Its journey took it straight to Ten Courts where it was judged. The King of the First Court directed it to the other courts to receive the requisite tortures and punishments as appropriate in each case. It was this journey that took 49 days.

While the soul at the shrine was the one most intimately connected with household routine and the one most frequently worshipped, its counterpart at the graveside had to make do with comparatively rare visits, once or at most twice a year. The Chinese visited grave sites at the spring festival known as the Qingming, or 'Clear and Bright'. It was also called the 'Grave-sweeping Festival', a time when the sites were cleaned and weeded. It was an occasion for the whole family who brought substantial offerings of food which then became

THE SAYINGS OF CONFUCIUS

CONFUCIUS (551-479 BC) was a poor, self-educated wandering Chinese scholar who lived through a period of warfare and anarchy. This led him to desire above all things a return to the unequal but orderly society he believed to have existed at the beginning of the Zhou dynasty, around the 11th century BC. Holding that a sound social order depended not on laws but on the personal qualities of those in power, Confucius hoped for the creation of a moral meritocracy: 'When rulers love to observe the rules of righteous behaviour, the common people respond readily to calls upon them for service.'

Confucius held that a person's moral strength was based on filial piety, which represented respect for authority and tradition and could be refined through the study of classical culture and the practice of moderation, loyalty, good manners and righteousness, all balanced by compassion. Respect for ancestors did not, therefore, represent a superstitious fear of ghosts but a proper sense of moral decorum: 'The superior man while his parents are alive, reverently serves them; and when they are dead, reverently sacrifices to them. His chief thought is how, to the end of life, not to disgrace them.'

Confucian thought was essentially optimistic, since it assumed that all men were basically good and an elite could strive for perfection. Even the worst could try to avoid disgracing their parents. For Confucius the truly good man pursued virtue for its own sake rather than for profit or utility.

Confucius claimed no originality as a thinker, presenting himself as a transmitter of old traditions. He was credited with writing or editing works of divination (the 'Book of Changes', *Yijing – I Ch'ing*), history (the 'Book of Documents') and music (the 'Book of Songs', *Shijing*). Sayings attributed to him and his disciples were collected as the 'Analects' (*Lunyu*).

Persecuted under the Qin dynasty (221-206 BC), Confucianism survived to be adopted as the major official belief system of the Han (206 BC-AD 220) and later Chinese dynasties. Under the Han, Confucius himself became the focus of a state-sponsored cult, a development he would surely have deplored.

By the 4th century Confucianism had spread to Korea and from there was transmitted to Japan. In practice, many of its assumptions such as the fear of anarchy, desirability of orthodoxy and respect for state functionaries, have continued under China's Communist regime, despite its theoretical rejection of the creed. More broadly, Confucian pragmatism and respect for learning, diligence and self-discipline have played a significant role in the economic progress of east Asian states, from Singapore through Vietnam, Hong Kong and Korea to Japan, in the 20th century.

THE BEAUTY OF RITUAL   A 19th-century statuette (right) portrays Confucius. The Sage sits with a group of disciples (below) in a scene of serenity that reflects his belief in the need for decorum in all settings.

the centrepiece for a graveside picnic. There was a less frequently observed festival in the autumn.

The choice of a grave site was dictated by *fengshui*, or geomancy. This was an elaborate procedure involving aspects of topography and astrology, as well as an artistic appreciation of an attractive setting. It was aimed at locating the precise spot that combined the most favourable influences likely to keep the ancestor's soul at peace. A good *fengshui* was also supposed to bring good fortune to the living family – health, wealth and happiness.

To fix such a position professional geomancers were employed, and they worked with special compasses, charts and voluminous texts. *Fengshui* was so important that poor families often 'stole' sites near the graves of prosperous families, hoping to get a share of their obvious good luck. And, since feuds between rival families were common, it was not unknown for villagers to deliberately deface their enemies' sites, by diverting streams or creating landslides so that the landscape was changed.

This meant that burial was not necessarily a once and for all event. Resiting was quite frequent and might take place years after the original burial. Indeed, some poor families had to make do with a quick, cheap burial while they saved up for a reburial more in keeping with their wishes for their ancestor and themselves, as well as more likely to impress the neighbours. A hurried burial was not at all seemly.

SUBSTITUTE ANCESTORS

The worship of ancestors was so important that even those who could not themselves produce offspring – and thus take their place in a family's continuity – still followed some of its trappings.

Among those who could not have an effective posterity were unmarried women. The Chinese had no place for them; there was not even a word for 'spinster'. The word they used meant 'girl not yet married'. Yet there were spinsters, women whose parents had been too poor to marry them off. In the usual course of events their souls would be condemned to an existence as wandering ghosts without the benefit of worship or sacrifice from later generations. Such women sometimes joined together in 'sisterhoods', and adopted ancestral practices.

BUDDHA'S BRETHREN
Beijing monks pose for the camera around 1865. With no physical offspring, monks and nuns relied on future generations of their successors to pay them their 'ancestral' dues.

BROTHERHOODS AND SECRET SOCIETIES

IN A SOCIETY dominated by ties of kinship or family, other groupings based on family style loyalties also flourished. Most such brotherhoods and sisterhoods were harmless. Often they involved regular meetings of like-minded people whose aim was to enjoy each other's company and give assistance to members in need.

Other associations were more sinister and were banned by governments frightened that they would become a focus for lawlessness. They included popular sects like the Yellow Heaven Sect which existed, despite the ban, throughout the centuries of Manchu rule and never, in fact, disturbed the peace. Most had some association with the arts of healing and taught the secrets of special diets, yogic meditation and 'spiritual' exercises like boxing and fencing.

As the 19th century dawned, however, rebellions multiplied. The White Lotus sect rose in revolt from 1796 to 1804, promising the return of the Buddha and the overthrow of the Manchu dynasty. It nearly bankrupted the government before it was defeated. In the 1850s rebels of the Taiping sect, influenced by Protestant Christianity, attempted to found a 'Heavenly Kingdom of Great Peace' and were only suppressed with foreign help. From 1898 to 1900 the violence of the followers of the society of the Righteous and Harmonious Fists – known in the West as the Boxers, after their belief in a boxing art thought to make them invulnerable – heralded the end of the empire itself.

Secret brotherhoods, meanwhile, included the Triads, who were founded in the 1670s and became active in opium smuggling and organised crime, as they are today.

BLOOD BROTHERS Taiping rebels attack Shanghai in the 1850s (left). The amulet (above), believed to confer protection on its owner from bullets, was taken from the body of a dead Boxer.

In the silk centres of Guangdong province in the south, there were several so-called 'old maid houses'. The silk industry opened new opportunities for female employment and so the sisters – women who were unmarried or had left their husbands – could earn their own livings. The 'old maid houses' provided a headquarters for ordinary activities but, most important, a home for their spirit tablets which would be worshipped by other members of the sisterhood after death. In a similar way, Buddhist or Taoist nuns worshipped former nuns and placed 'ancestral' tablets on 'ancestral' altars.

Other classes deprived of descendants included eunuchs, thousands of whom were employed at the Imperial Court. They felt the loss of their ancestral line deeply, and compensated for the lack of a true lineage in much the same way as nuns. In the words of a writer in the late 19th century: 'As eunuchs, after death, cannot be sacrificed to by their children – they have none – the government allows a yearly sum to enable a certain number of eunuchs to go to the cemeteries in the spring and autumn to burn paper money, and offer sacrifices at the tombs of those who have been buried there.'

THE SUPREME 'PARENT'
One effect of ancestor worship was to reinforce deference to authority throughout Chinese society. This was powerfully demonstrated by the veneration given everywhere to the most important

THE ULTIMATE MARK OF RESPECT

TO THE EMPEROR, as the 'Son of Heaven', was owed the most extreme form of self-abasement, the kowtow or *ketou*, literally 'knock the head [on the ground]'. Father Ripa, an Italian Jesuit, recorded his own first presentation to the Guangxu Emperor, who reigned from 1875 to 1908:

❝ Upon his right and left were some European missionaries . . . They had their feet close together and their arms were hanging down, which in China is a sign of modesty and respect. Following the instructions we received from the mandarins, as soon as we were within sight of the Emperor, we hastened our steps to his divan . . . and there we stood a few moments, with closed feet and arms hanging down. Then, at a signal given by the master of ceremonies lowering his hand, we bent our knees. After remaining a short time in this position, at another signal we inclined our heads slowly till we touched the ground with the forehead. This was repeated a second and third time. After these three prostrations we rose to our feet, and then we again repeated them in the same manner, till they amounted to nine [a 'perfect' number]. This homage is called the great or solemn ceremony. ❞

'parent' of all – the emperor. His subjects as obedient children thus owed him the reverence due to a supreme parent, just as he in his turn owed ultimate respect to the King of Heaven to whom he alone could make sacrificial offerings.

The emperor worshipped the ultimate ancestor at the Temple of Heaven in Beijing. Set in glorious parkland, it was circular, triple-terraced and its domes gleamed in heaven's sacred blue. Here at the time of the Winter Solstice, the most solemn sacrifice of all was made. The emperor prepared himself for this rite with a penitential fast of three days and nights, the last of which was spent in a Purifying Palace in the temple enclosure. He arrived in a carriage drawn by elephants and attended by high-ranking visitors and nobles.

When the great day dawned he dressed in sacrificial robes and was borne to the awesome steps made of white marble that led to the lowest terrace of the temple. When he reached the second terrace a ritual sacrifice was enacted. An unblemished two-year-old bullock was killed and its carcass burned.

ON ALL FOURS The emperor (below) holds an audience. An official clutches a *hu* (right and below right), an ivory wand held before the mouth when addressing the emperor.

Then he mounted to the third and highest terrace, kneeling in the centre of a series of marble circles which, in multiples of nine, patterned the floor. There he offered incense, jade cups and silk, prostrating himself nine times – nine was regarded as a 'perfect' number – before a sacred shrine. Around him his attendants performed a ritual dance and played ritual music. Finally, still on his knees, he accepted 'flesh of happiness' and 'a cup of happiness' from one of his attendants, prostrating himself three more times.

LIFE IN TOWN AND COUNTRY

與簞食亭午來餉婦要兒知

稼穡豈日事攜幼

At the height of its prosperity in the late 17th and early 18th centuries Qing China had the world's largest cities, notably Beijing with a population of some 700 000 – London's population in 1700 was around 600 000. Even so, the overwhelming majority of the Qing emperors' subjects lived in the countryside. The villages supplied the cities with food and raw materials and cheap migrant labour. In return they received manufactured goods along with refuse and rubbish to fertilise their fields.

SURVIVING IN THE CITY

Chinese city life was busy, smelly and competitive. Shops lined the streets, with whole streets

given over to one speciality, such as silks, books, toys, fireworks, meat, fish, furniture or

porcelain. Homes were low buildings hidden behind walls and arranged around courtyards.

CHINESE CITIES were, ideally, squares within square walls. According to one classical Chinese text, the *Zhou li*, dating from around 200 BC, there should be 'nine meridional and nine latitudinal avenues [inside the walls of a well-planned city], each of the former being nine chariot tracks in width'. Such a layout was not just a remarkably early example of town planning. It was a religious symbol, reflecting the belief that the Earth itself was a square, with China's emperor ruling from its centre – the importance of nine was that it was regarded as a 'perfect' number. Beijing and Chang'an (modern Xi'an in central China, and the capital of the Tang dynasty from AD 618 to 906) were two cities that approximated closely to this classical ideal, and nearly all centres of any significance were walled and basically square in layout where topography permitted.

This relative uniformity meant, at first sight, a certain drabness. At the end of the 18th century the British diplomat Sir John Barrow described Beijing: 'The first appearance of this celebrated capital is not much calculated to raise high expectations, nor does it in the least improve upon a more intimate acquaintance. In approaching a European city it generally happens that a great variety of objects catch the eye, [such] as the towers and spires of churches, domes, obelisks and other buildings for public purposes towering above the rest; and the mind is amused in conjecturing the form and magnitude of their several constructions, and the uses to which they may be applied . . . In [Beijing] not even a chimney is seen rising above the roofs of the houses which, being all nearly of the same height, and the streets laid out in straight lines, have the appearance and the regularity of a large encampment.'

Other visitors revealed that Chinese cities behind their apparent uniformity were

CITY STRENGTH Stout walls both guaranteed and symbolised the security of a city. When its fortifications were in decay it was a sure sign that the city, too, was declining. These are the gates of a provincial capital visited by the Kangxi Emperor (1662-1722).

continued on page 50

WHERE TO BUY YOUR MEDICINE
Physic Street in Guangzhou (Canton) was where herbalists and other medical specialists clustered together.

without mutual concession. The spectacle of a portly gentleman walking sideways for a few paces because he is a few inches less broad from front to back than he is from side to side, is one that appears after a little time to be very natural and not at all humorous.'

THE LURE OF THE CITY

Administratively, the Chinese Empire was divided into 18 provinces, many of them as large as European kingdoms and each with its own administrative capital. The cities attracted tradespeople from throughout the surrounding countryside. The provincial centres also received an influx of students every

far from orderly and harmonious. The 19th-century British missionary Edwin Dukes carefully enjoined his readers to 'put away, if you please, all the prejudices you have acquired from childhood in connection with the word "street" '.

He continued: 'Imagine the streets as mere alleys and courts, and not at all what we mean by the word "street". Stretch out your arms, and reflect that, in so doing, in an ordinary Chinese town, you would generally be able to touch the counters of the shops on both sides of the way. Many towns, of course, have a few streets twice, and even three times, that width; but they are the exception, while on the other hand, there is in every populous town an immense network of narrow alleys in which it is impossible for two persons to pass one another

STREETS AT RIGHT ANGLES   A plan of Beijing in 1843 reveals the classic grid pattern of Chinese cities. This was both symbolic and functional, with different activities assigned to different areas.

HIGHWAY TO HEAVEN

BOTH SIDES of Beijing's Centre Street are lined with stalls from which appetising smells waft across the thoroughfare tempting passing travellers to sample a snack. On the left a kite-seller displays his wares; on the right a street barber shaves a customer's head, while nearby him children gather to gawp at a puppet show. Fortunetellers and letter-writers also ply their trades by the wayside. Beggars are regularly chased away and just as regularly return for alms. Peasants carrying baskets on yokes bring in fresh produce from the countryside. Others use wheelbarrows, an ancient Chinese invention. Larger loads are brought by covered two-wheeled carts. The leisured classes pass by in traditional sedan chairs or new-fangled rickshaws. At night, when the stalls are shut up, the silence will be broken by the wheels of foul-smelling 'honey carts' which tour the city, draining cesspits and vats to carry their contents out to the farms beyond the city walls.

A PROFESSIONAL BEGGAR

UNLIKE THE BLIND, who lived by singing or telling fortunes, or the crippled, widowed and orphaned, who begged piteously at street corners as the only alternative to starvation, Li Wan, a fit and sturdy man in his thirties, begged because it was his chosen profession.

His bedroom might be a culvert beneath the city walls, but he regarded half a dozen of the city's prosperous streets as so many rooms in his personal mansion. Far from slinking in the shadows, he strode along boldly and was all too well known to the traders.

Usually sleeping off the dreams induced by opium or rice wine, Li saw no point in stirring himself before

mid-morning, when business was in full swing. Generally he had only to appear at the door of a shop for a young assistant to spring forward with a small coin which he would pocket briskly as

CALL TO ALMS
A professional beggar clacks a rattle as he makes his plea for charity. Although clad in tatters, he still carries a fan.

his due. The alternative, as the shopkeeper knew from past experience, was a brief silence, followed by a noisy invasion by Li, backed up by comrades who usually worked other districts. Screaming, spitting, banging pots and waving rattles and cudgels, they would drive every customer out within seconds. Of course, the shopkeeper could go to the magistrate – but the delays, the tips, the gifts . . . It was easier – and far cheaper – just to pay up.

And Li, as a professional, stuck to his side of the bargain. Once paid he fixed a small red ticket beside the shop entrance to serve as both a receipt and a warning to other beggars to keep off. For a few days, at least, peace would reign in the street of the silk-vendors. . . .

three years to sit the all-important state examinations that were an essential step on the path towards becoming a mandarin. There were grander visitors, too. The Kangxi (K'ang-hsi) Emperor, in particular, who reigned from 1662 to 1722, toured local provinces on a number of occasions and stayed in the local capitals such as Suzhou, Nanjing (Nanking) and Yangzhou.

The chaos and congestion in the streets was immediately and constantly commented on. On arriving in Beijing in 1697 the Neapolitan traveller Gemelli Careri wrote: 'We had a great deal of trouble today because of the multitude of carts, camels, and mares which go to [Beijing] and return from it, and which is so large that one has difficulty in moving.'

Little more than half a century later the French priest Father du Halde commented on the 'innumerable multitude of people who fill these streets and the congestion caused by the surprising quantity of horses, mules, asses, camels, carts, wagons and chairs . . .' Adding to the confusion, he

observed, were 'various groups, 100 or 200 strong, who gather here and there to listen to fortune-tellers, conjurers, singers and others reading or telling some tale conducive to laughter or pleasure, or even to charlatans who distribute their remedies and demonstrate the wonderful effects thereof. People who are not of the common run would be stopped every moment if they were not preceded by a horseman who pushes back the crowd, warning them to make way.'

Foreigners also united in recoiling from the smell. The Chinese did not wear underclothes and slept in the same clothes they wore by day. Nor did they bother too much with washing. Another source of the stench was euphemistically known as 'night soil'. Sir John Barrow was at first puzzled by the carts full of 'dry brown cakes not much larger but thicker than those we call crumpets'. But he soon realised that they were made from animal and human excrement, collected in every city, dried for transporting and used in gardens and farms all over China.

The Chinese never troubled about water closets; they simply collected their waste in earthen jugs while thousands of men and children scraped a living by collecting rubbish from the streets. It was a surprisingly profitable business, but, less surprisingly, according to Barrow, 'though the city is cleared of its filth, it seldom loses its fragrance'.

EASY SHOPPING

It was customary for the large houses or palaces of the rich to have only one large gate onto the street, flanked by two fairly low buildings occupied by servants, tradespeople and other workers. City streets were thus mostly lined with booths and shops which had tall poles, often decorated with cloth streamers, holding up their signboards.

This way of ordering things made for convenience, as another Catholic priest, Father de

STEP THIS WAY, PLEASE The shopowner Linchong in Guangzhou (Canton) entices a European customer into his premises. The wares in his 'basket shop' include baskets, boxes, trays, mats and hats.

Magaillans, noted: 'A good part of the streets in our [European] towns are lined with the houses of wealthy people; and one is thus obliged to go a very long way to the market or the ports to obtain necessary articles, while in [Beijing] – and it is the same in all the other towns of China – everything one could want to buy for maintenance, subsistence and even more for pleasure, is to be found at one's doorstep, because these small houses are shops, taverns or stalls.'

Homes were mostly single-storeyed. Substantial ones spread outwards rather than upwards, with a number of apartments linked to courtyards and enclosed behind walls. The uniform lowness was a characteristic of all Chinese building, emphasised in Beijing where it was unthinkable for anyone to contemplate constructing a mansion higher than the emperor's palace.

Of course, for every large house with its multiple apartments and courtyards, there were many

RECYCLING Little was wasted in Chinese cities. Men like these were employed to make regular collections of refuse which helped to limit disease and provided raw materials for makers of paper and coarse cloth.

thousands of one-roomed hovels accommodating whole families, engaged in a precarious mixture of farming and handicrafts to eke out their existence. Here families lived amidst scurrying chickens, grunting pigs and ubiquitous mangy dogs, since even in the greatest cities rural life was never far away. Large areas of cultivation were often enclosed within the city walls. Many families grew subsistence crops on small patches of ground around their homes, hoping to sell surpluses at the markets.

For most city-dwellers, like their country cousins, the daily round was an effort to sell whatever they had – their skills, brawn, ingenuity – for a few coppers. Foreign observers remarked on the numbers of itinerant workers – masons, carpenters, blacksmiths and so on – all eagerly pressing their services on whoever showed any interest in

them. The foreigners' eyes were particularly caught by all that was most colourful and, for them, unusual in the city scenes. They wondered at the number and display of coffin shops; at the skills of innumerable barbers who whisked hair away from the crowns of clients' heads with all the panache of expert swordsmen; at the prevalence of fortune-tellers and of acrobats and jugglers entertaining the crowds; at the elaborate kites; at the indefatigable rickshaw boys (the biggest single occupation in any large city); at the throngs of beggars around temple courtyards; at shops devoted to paper effigies for funerals, fireworks, delicate moving fans and toys of every description.

PAYING IN COPPER AND PAYING IN SILVER

Paying for what you bought in Chinese cities was rarely a simple operation. There were two different currency systems, one copper and the other silver. Copper was used for making small payments and shopping, silver for large transactions. But they were unrelated, and only copper was controlled by the government.

The single copper coin was called a 'cash'. It was cumbersome and heavy to carry in bulk. Moreover, when the amount of copper was reduced by the government (through mixing it with baser metals) or worn down through use, it lost value. People carried them in strings of 1000, a laborious task because each string had to be carefully graded and neatly arranged in order of size and copper content – the coins had a hole in the middle and were strung on a string. Usually this job was done at a moneychanging shop which charged, typically, 10 per cent for doing so. The endless haggling that characterised most transactions was more often than not an argument about what a string of cash was actually worth.

The Chinese did not give a monetary value to gold. From the 15th century onwards, however, merchants showed an increasing preference for silver over copper as a means of exchange, leading to a massive influx of the metal into China. In time the state, too, came to favour silver for the payment of taxes. The basic unit was the *tael*, equivalent to 1 oz (30 g) of silver. The metal was imported from Japan or, from the 1560s onwards, across the Pacific from the Americas via the Spanish-ruled

As Good as . . . Silver

CHINESE GOVERNMENTS began experimenting with paper money as far back as 1024. Early notes were limited to certain regions and were valid only for a limited period of time. In 1260, however, China's Mongol conquerors began to issue the first 'national' paper currency with an extended life. The Chinese also used forms of cheques, promissory notes and bills of exchange centuries before they were known in the West.

The system was well enough managed to survive for some 200 years until it was undermined by the uncontrolled, inflationary use of the printing press to churn out more and more money. The last notes before modern times were issued in 1643 on the eve of the fall of the Ming dynasty. Their Qing successors equated paper money with bad administration and would have none of it.

In the late Qing era, radical changes in the relative world values of copper, silver and gold greatly aggravated China's growing miseries. This happened as 19th-century Western countries generally adopted the gold standard as the basis for their different currencies. At the same time, as tensions heightened between Western traders and the Chinese authorities, the Western nations squeezed hundreds of millions of pounds of silver out of China in indemnities for alleged damage to their property.

The poor who held most of China's copper currency found that it halved in value against silver (the other chief form of currency) between 1820 and 1845 – but they still had to pay their taxes in silver. The Chinese government suffered from foreign predators and creditors, as the value of silver against the gold-backed US dollar halved between 1887 and 1902 alone. Inflation, corruption, tax evasion and widespread smuggling were the almost inevitable result of these disastrous trends.

Philippines. Historians have estimated that as much as a half the silver mined in the Americas between 1527 and 1821 found its way to China. Silver dollars and pesos minted in Mexico continued in circulation into the 20th century – to the Chinese they were just pieces of silver and were weighed as if raw metal.

The relationship between the silver and copper currencies was never fixed and became a frequent cause of confusion and disputes. At grass-roots level barter of essential goods continued to be practised.

DRAMAS OF EVERYDAY LIFE

The Chinese people's own view of urban life was vividly depicted in a 17th-century novel *The Romance of the Three Teachings*. This gave intimate descriptions of the lives and problems of people in the increasingly urbanised region of south-east China around the lower Chang Jiang (Yangtze) basin. In the novel, urban life in the growing commercial centres is colourfully evoked: shopkeepers know all the gossip and loud marketplace squabbles provide plenty to gossip about. In this anonymous urban setting young wastrels dissipate family fortunes in whoring and gambling; sycophants sponge off the rich; phony literati while away their days in poetry, oblivious to the human dramas going on around them. The *continued on page 56*

CASHING IN A moneylender (left) with his stock-in-trade – strings of coins, known as cash. An elegantly robed Guangzhou merchant (above), depicted around 1795, is dressed for the street.

THE PRINCE OF POTTERY

Hardness, whiteness, smoothness and translucence are

hallmarks of true porcelain – a Chinese invention.

THE ESSENTIAL ingredient of porcelain is kaolin, a white clay which is an aluminium silica compound. It takes its name from Gaoling ('high hill'), where it was first found, 20 miles (32 km) from the kiln centre at Jingdezhen in southern China. Kaolin was mentioned as a medicinal drug (it is still used as a stomach-settler) long before it was referred to in connection with pottery.

A primitive form of true porcelain was produced in China under the Tang dynasty (618-906 AD). Then, under the Song emperors (960-1279), came one of the supreme flowerings of the Chinese potters' art. In the north, porcelain-makers produced delicate white pots exquisitely ornamented with incised patterns of birds, fish and plants. In the south, Jingdezhen – inaugurated as an official porcelain-making centre by imperial decree around 1005 – manufactured fine white porcelain with a delicate bluish glaze.

MUSCLE POWER A potter in this watercolour throws a gigantic vase on a wheel. One man carries away a vase. Another brings two large lumps of clay hanging from a yoke.

Porcelain as we now tend to think of it – with glazed designs in different colours – dates first from the 14th century when China was ruled by the Mongol Yuan dynasty. By then the greatly expanded kilns at Jingdezhen

were producing the fine blue-and-white ware – using cobalt to create the blue patterns – that would become synonymous with China. They were decorated with a multitude of designs including plants, flowers, birds, legendary and real animals and scenes from dramas.

Refinements continued under the Ming emperors (1368-1644), and in the 15th century the custom of placing a reign mark on the base of pots produced for the imperial household was introduced. Designs became less stylised and more pictorial. Later in the Ming era new

PORCELAIN PRODUCTION LINE The man in the foreground is painting decorative motifs in cobalt. The one behind him paints rings around the rims, and the two on the right glaze bowls ready for firing.

techniques meant porcelain-makers could make freer use of colours other than blue.

Outside China, the first definite mention of Chinese porcelain comes from an Arab traveller, Suleyman, in 851 AD. The Islamic world was swift to embrace it as a luxury import but it did not appear in western Europe until the 15th century. After that, exports to Europe boomed, notably via the Dutch East India Company.

True porcelain was produced for the first time in Europe in 1709, by accident, when the experimenter Frederick Böttger discovered that his wig-powder contained kaolin. His patron, Augustus of Saxony, immediately established a royal factory at Meissen, which was soon followed by others at Dresden and Sèvres. Delft in Holland became famous for its blue-

and-white wares, a direct imitation of classic Ming patterns.

An English potter Josiah Spode experimented successfully to produce 'bone china', a porcelain which incorporated calcium phosphate obtained from roasting cattle bones. Easier to produce than Chinese porcelain and less prone to chipping, this displaced the original product in Britain and the USA.

Chinese exporters responded to the challenge of European manufacture by turning out products decorated with European motifs or heraldic coats of arms. But the volume of exports from centres such as Jingdezhen fell off during the 18th century.

Within China itself during the Qing period, multicoloured enamel decoration became popular, featuring such novel colorations as 'eel-skin yellow', 'snakeskin green' and 'peach bloom'. Critics took it as a sign of deteriorating standards of connoisseurship that courtiers began demanding porcelain imitations of ancient bronzes and porcelain versions of such objects as musical instruments and revolving boxes. The chaotic conditions of the 19th century severely disrupted the Chinese industry and the quality of its output declined.

CLASSIC LINES Blue-and-white bowls like this were characteristic of the late Ming and early Qing periods. Water transport (right) helped to reduce losses from breakages.

THE MOST PRIZED POSSESSION

FEW CRAFTSMEN stood higher in the esteem of Chinese connoisseurs than workers in jade – a substance they prized beyond gold or any precious gem. Believing jade to be indestructible, the Chinese attributed to it a mystical power to prevent decay and ward off evil.

Jade is the name given to two unrelated mineral compounds, both so hard that a steel knife leaves no mark on them. It is, therefore, not carved but ground with an abrasive compound – and great patience. Commonly thought of as green, jade comes, in fact, in many shades from white to black. Nephrite, the more common form, has been used in China to make grave goods, jewellery, weapons and ceremonial items since 2000 BC. Jadeite, even harder than nephrite, became available from Burma after around 1780.

Jade 'carving', an art that had fallen into relative neglect, greatly revived under the Qing. Their craftsmen used it to make everything from vases and bowls to toggles and brush-rests in the shape of mountain ranges – symbols of longevity.

RIVER OF DREAMS
A jade fishing boat, with crew and cat, would remind its owner of the pleasures of a simple life.

---

towns are shown to be peopled with entrepreneurs of all kinds from wealthy salt dealers to lowly peddlers while beneath the entrepreneurs is a criminal underclass of thieves, prostitutes and runaway servants. Rich and poor are all struggling to get ahead in a fiercely competitive environment where money and influence are replacing traditional values as the standards of behaviour. Learning and virtue count for little in a world where people are trying to get rich, stay rich or just pretend to be rich.

Guilds provided an important social focus. In part these reflected the refusal of most Chinese people to see themselves as individuals, seeking instead some group within which to submerge their identities. The guilds were not unlike medieval European ones: associations of merchants or craftsmen preserving a monopoly and trying to regulate the quality of goods, prices, weights and measures. Such guilds also offered help for marriage and funeral expenses and served as informal meeting houses.

Peculiar to Beijing with its great population of officials was the large number of

guilds representing every province and district in China, well over 1000 in all. Here, those from Fuzhou (Foochow), Guangzhou (Canton) or other cities could lodge and socialise with fellow 'locals', paying nothing because they were financed from

HITTING THE NOTE Strolling musicians entertain a family of passers-by. Other popular street diversions included boxing matches, wrestling and cockfighting – quails and locusts were also used for fighting.

ART AND ARTIFICE The gardens of the imperial Summer Palace just outside Beijing were artfully laid out to afford a variety of vistas and viewpoints. Right: Ladies play *go*, a sophisticated game of strategy which appeals strongly to the mathematical mind.

the home territory. Being 'local' was not always the same as the place you came from: you could, for instance, be born and brought up in the city of Nanjing but you were not considered a native there if your ancestors had their origin in another part of China.

AT THE THEATRE

For both visitors and locals, a rich variety of entertainments was available. By far the most popular were theatricals. Many performances were 'private' – held by hosts to entertain guests in their homes or at restaurants. Most restaurants had one or two 'theatres'; usually these were no more than open spaces with room for the mat which served as a stage. Other performances might be given to thank the rain god for rain, or an earth god for a good harvest.

Public theatres were rarely fixed sites – a few poles for a mat roof and a printed backdrop as scenery was all that was needed, apart from benches for the audience. Plays were normally historical dramas of legendary sagas or 'morality' tales about dissolute sons redeeming themselves through filial piety or wise judges reconciling enemies. Acting was highly stylised, mostly in high falsetto with innumerable pauses for gong beats, music and songs. There were no actresses since men took the female parts. Plays were not long – half an hour or so – but performances consisted of up to half a dozen of these; a cycle of such plays lasted several days. The audiences were constantly interrupted by 'cushion

REBEL THEATRICALS

Popular theatre took such a hold on the imagination of ordinary Chinese people that during the Boxer Rising of 1899-1900 many of the rebels spoke in theatrical rhetoric and claimed the magic powers which were the stock-in-trade of stage fantasy.

men', 'tea men', programme-sellers and others. Marionette theatres and shadow plays were, if anything, more popular still.

Gambling was another all-absorbing diversion. 'No Chinaman is without dice or cards', commented Barrow. If cards were not available, the game of fingers was widespread, particularly among the poor. Barrow noted the form of play: 'Two persons, sitting directly opposite to each other, raise their hands at the same moment, when each calls out the number he guesses to be the sum of the fingers expanded by himself and his adversary. The closed fist is none, the thumb one, the thumb and forefinger two [and so on], so that the chances lie between 0 and 5 as each must know the number held out by himself.' A variation on this game was played by 'the middling class of people when . . . the loser is always obliged to drink off a cup of wine'.

More intellectually demanding was the game of *weiqi* played by scholars. This was a fiendishly difficult game, related to chess but played on a board with 320 squares with the object of building walls and protecting them while simultaneously attacking those of your opponent. (Mah-jong, which became popular in the West in the 1920s, was a comparative upstart of a game, probably dating back no further than the late 19th century.)

More sensual urban pleasures were offered by 'houses of ill-repute', frowned on by missionaries, but carrying little stigma for the Chinese. There were plenty of these, patronised by scholar-officials and the lower classes alike. Some were home to the famous 'sing-song' girls who were experts in

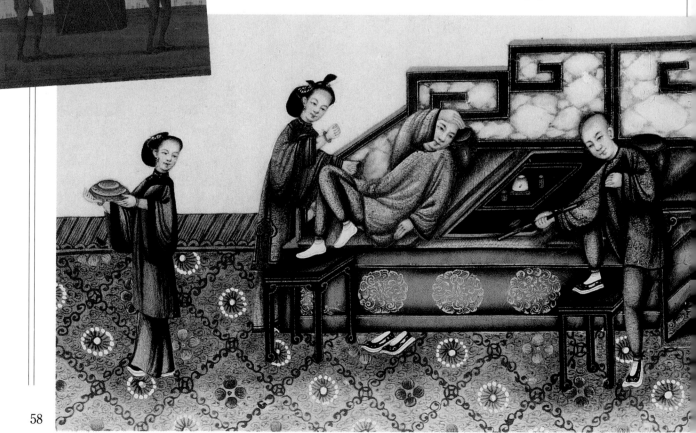

CLOUDING THE MIND Indian porters (left) tote a case of opium. Addicts (below) seek temporary oblivion in an opium den. By 1890 there may have been 15 million opium addicts in China – about 10 per cent of the population.

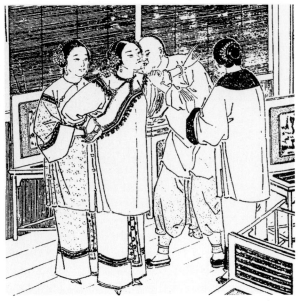

DO YOUR DESIRE Prostitutes stand with a client. Few such girls could hope to escape from what was little better than slavery, except through the patronage of a wealthy man who might take one as a concubine.

massage and sometimes had the social skills to accompany well-to-do clients as escorts.

Opium dens rapidly mushroomed in every city during the later Qing era. One observer estimated that by the late 19th century there were some 170 dens in Tianjin (Tientsin); more than 1000 in Hangzhou; more than 1200 shops and dens in Chongqing. Certainly by the end of the century opium was everywhere – sold in dens and shops as well as by itinerant traders at wayside stalls, especially during the annual fairs and festivals. For these events, the peddlers would set up their booths near the temples in advance of the festivities and then sell to the holiday crowds who came in from the countryside.

A RISING POPULATION

The Chinese population had risen rapidly in the 18th and 19th centuries, from something like 143 million in 1743 to 360 million by 1812. Of these an increasing number were city-dwellers, with the growth of industries as well as trade bringing many into the urban centres. These included the great silk and satin-producing centres such as Suzhou and Nanjing around the Chang Jiang (Yangtze) delta, which even in the 18th century had as many as 30 000 satin looms alone. The porcelain ovens of Jingdezhen in Jiangxi employed tens of thousands of ceramic craftsmen, while the coastal province of Fujian (Fukien) was a centre for both paper and sugar manufacture. As foreign trade opened up, so coastal cities and ports, such as Guangzhou (Canton) and Shanghai expanded.

Nonetheless, the proportion of Chinese people living in cities remained low. Even by the end of the 19th century, scholars estimate that no more than 6 per cent of the population lived in centres with more than 200 000 inhabitants. Daily life for the vast majority of Chinese people remained rooted firmly in the villages and countryside.

EYEWITNESS

A CHAPTER OF DISASTERS FOR TANCHENG

TANCHENG, an unremarkable city in Shandong province, suffered so many catastrophes in the mid 17th century that its local historian concluded that it was as if fate itself had decided to 'throw rocks at a man who had already fallen down a well'. Peasant rebellions in the 1620s, banditry in the 1630s, locusts in 1640, a Manchu raid in 1643, more bandit raids in 1648, 1650 and 1651, floods in 1649, 1651 and 1659 culminated in even greater disasters in the 1660s:

❛ For 30 years now fields have lain under flood water or weeds; we still cannot bear to speak of all the devastation. On top of this came the famine of 1665; and after the earthquake of 1668 not a single ear of grain was harvested, over half the people were dying of starvation, their homes were all destroyed and 10 000 men and women were crushed to death in the ruins. Those who were left wept with hunger and cold by day, and slept out in the open country by night. Fathers and sons could not help each other, neighbours could not protect each other. The old and the weak moved from ditch to ditch, the young and strong all fled to other areas. Travellers passing through were moved to tears by what they saw. . . . ❜

FARM AND VILLAGE

China's huge population survived on a diet of grains, vegetables and fish. The farmer and

the fisherman, rather than the hunter or the herdsmen, filled the nation's stomach.

Cultivation was intensive, taking advantage of every scrap of available land.

CHINA was a land of farmers without farms – as people in the West understand a farm. There was no tradition of primogeniture, so inherited land was divided equally among sons. Generations of such divisions, haphazard purchasing as opportunities arose, forced selling due to poverty and, above all, a massive population increase from the 1680s onwards, had all combined to create a patchwork landscape of tiny fields.

Peasant farms averaged only 3 or 4 acres (1.2 or 1.6 ha) each, and these were divided into even smaller parcels, scattered over any area within walking and working distance. Vast regions of valley and hillside all over China were carved up into narrow tiers by terracing – many of these strips covering no more than the size of a carpet or

tablecloth – thereby making the best possible use of every scrap of suitable land. Farming in such circumstances is better described as a form of perpetual, ever-vigilant, exhausting and backbreaking market gardening.

There were few farm animals. A family might keep a couple of chickens and perhaps a pig which could sniff out its own food and was valuable for manure. Some farmers kept an ox or a mule to pull their ploughs. Oxen, very occasionally a horse, or possibly a camel in the north, were likely to be the extent of a peasant's help with hauling and carrying, and many lacked even these. Foreigners were surprised to see men and even women yoked to the plough, sometimes alongside an ox. The wheelbarrow was the implement that, more than any other, helped to lighten the farmer's load. In the Chinese version, it often had a rope to loop around the neck to help support the weight.

The peasantry worked the land. Some members of the smaller, local gentry lived in the country, but the wealthy preferred the comforts of urban life and had no ambition to be 'gentlemen farmers'. A handful of the rich, a few large groups of families and some temples did own up to 1000 acres (400 ha), but they were exceptional. Moreover, these colossal (by Chinese standards) landowners did not employ labourers to work their estates as integrated units but commonly rented their land in small parcels to scores or hundreds of peasant families. There was no established landed aristocracy with a tradition of country-house living, able to reserve vast tracts of land for hunting, shooting and fishing.

Cattle and dairy farming were also unknown through most of China, above all the south. With

LIFE IN THE COMPOUND All the family are kept busy in a farm compound. A telltale sign of poverty is the roof, only half tiled, with the rest covered with thatch.

TAKING THE STRAIN Few peasants could afford draught animals to work their land. If they did have one, its death or injury was a major catastrophe.

land at such a premium, stock raising was far too extravagant a use to put it to. Rice and grain were much more productive, particularly in large areas of flat land. The south was also too wet to be very suitable for stock. The only areas with enough pasture were the northern border regions such as Mongolia where nomads moved around with their cattle and the lower mountain regions of the interior where the goat-like Chinese sheep were able to negotiate the terrain and find herbage for themselves.

Elsewhere, the sheer intensity of rural activity impressed foreigners. Writing near the start of the Qing period, one Jesuit missionary was amazed that 'there was not an inch of land ... not the smallest corner that was not cultivated'. A hundred years later another Jesuit wrote: 'All the plains are cultivated. One sees neither hedges, ditches, nor almost any trees, so afraid are they of leaving an inch of land [untilled].' This picture was common through most of China, whether in the drier north where the land was covered with wheat, millet and maize, or in the teeming wetlands of the south where the people depended on rice.

RICE THE PROVIDER

Rice fed China; for nine-tenths of the population it provided nine-tenths of their diet. It was a wonder crop which could provide two, in places even three, harvests a year. Modern historians have estimated that an acre of land devoted to rice could produce food energy of more than 2.9 million calories (7.25 million calories for 1 ha). This compared with 0.4 million calories for an acre of wheat and only 137 600 calories from

PADDY PARADE Rice seedlings are planted out in regimented rows to make maximum use of the richly fertilised mass of water, soil, dung, urine and other wastes.

61

meat if an acre of land was used for stock-raising. New strains of rice were introduced from the West in the 18th century – along with crops that had never been seen in China before such as the sweet potato and peanut from South America.

Rice is one of the most labour-intensive of crops and took a terrible toll on the farmer. Wherever there was double or triple cropping – in more than three-quarters of China's rice lands – there was no time to plant seeds in the fields. The farmer grew his young shoots in seedbeds and then hauled them across to his scattered patches of land at planting time. Carrying these loads was daunting, and planting in sodden fields even more so. But this was only a fraction of the peasant's labour. Young shoots from the beds had to be planted the moment one of the two – or three – harvests had been gathered; this in itself was a massive task for one man.

Then the fields needed to be drained, ploughed, levelled, manured and reflooded before replanting.

Fertilising with mud, ash and both human and animal 'night soil' was a ceaseless activity on fields which had to remain rich and productive for generation after generation. There was a relentless need to adjust water levels – fields were crisscrossed with irrigation canals and water was raised by bucket or by a machine consisting of a series of buckets, worked on a treadle. Protecting the crop from blight and insect pests called for further ceaseless labour.

No less than 60 tons of manure per acre (148 tons per hectare) often had to be mixed into the soil in the course of a year, while a peasant might well need to raise 300 tons of water per acre (740 tons per hectare) per day to ensure that his crop survived. And, of course, while all this was happening in preparation for the new harvest, the recent one

MAKING THE MOST OF THINGS The farmer, like the craftsman, made do with simple technology. Peasants gather water from an irrigation canal and tip it down a 'cascade' of rush matting to top up the water level in a rice-paddy (left). Others stack the harvest (above).

THE WIND WATER MAN – PROSPECTING FOR PROSPERITY

IT WAS ALREADY MIDMORNING when Lin entered the village, but he had been busy since sunrise, pacing briskly through the surrounding hills and squinting at the settlement from various vantage points. Now he walked slowly, pausing occasionally to look round and note the location of such features as the village pond, a grove of trees, a wayside shrine and the cemetery. Unhurriedly Lin approached his client's home, which looked as though it had seen better days.

The client, Wei, greeted him with the grave but self-satisfied air of a man who has come into a more substantial inheritance than he had anticipated – which was, indeed, the case. Lin saw at a glance from Wei's elegant robe that the long period of formal mourning was now over but a staid decorum still governed their interview, emphasising Wei's new status as the head of a large household. The men exchanged lengthy pleasantries and drank several cups of tea before Wei delicately raised the subject of business – how the splendid new house he proposed to build himself should be aligned.

Like his father and grandfather before him, Lin had studied *feng-shui* ('wind water') since childhood. Mastery of his craft rested on a knowledge of complex techniques for measuring coordinates of time and space and a finely balanced combination of intuition and diplomacy. As everybody knew, the Earth, like the human body, was veined with winding channels through which its life force pulsated. The site where these converged would prove auspicious for a dwelling place – for this life or the next.

Disruptive influences, especially man-made straight lines such as roads or ditches, could provide a highway (carefully broken in city streets with special gates) along which malevolent forces could travel. This allowed them to wreak havoc in the lives of humans by destroying their harmony with the patterns and rhythms of Heaven and Earth.

Diffidently, Lin requested confirmation of the details of Wei's hour and place of birth. It was information he already possessed; indeed, he could hardly have got this far without it. But he liked to impress clients with attention to detail. For the same reason he made a show of manipulating a complex compass. Then he excused himself, left the verandah and stood in the courtyard, peering along the line of a drainage ditch running through a neighbouring field.

'Pointed as a dagger', he murmured just loud enough to be heard as he remounted the verandah. Wei looked up anxiously and confirmed that it had been recently dug by the field's owner. Lin feigned polite surprise at what he was sure was an unwittingly hostile act, although he knew full well that no love was lost between the overweening Wei and his neighbour.

Reassuringly he advised the planting of a protective screen of seven saplings, and then proceeded

SPOT ON A geomancer and his assistants determine the luckiest location for a new house – with a protective hill behind and a flowing stream in front.

to sketch out with handsome brush strokes his recommendations for the alignment of the new mansion. He took his time, partly to underline the value of his mysterious powers and partly because he expected to share the pleasures of Wei's table if he could make the task last until evening. It was not just self-indulgence. Wei in his cups would surely be agreeable to discussing the important matter of choosing the correct site for his father's permanent tomb.

needed threshing, stacking and packing before it could be transported by land or water.

Double or triple cropping was often varied with the cultivation of alternative grains. In the south, two rice crops might be interspersed with one of wheat; in the north one of wheat with one of cotton or soya beans. Rarely was there a fallow season during which the land could be peaceably grazed by livestock, giving the farmer a well-earned rest. On the contrary, the farmer depended on the constant sweat of his brow and the strength of his arms, along with all the help his wife and children could give him.

The peasants' tools were primitive in the extreme. They normally consisted of a plough, which was little more than a simple share – or cutting blade – fixed to bamboo rods, a hoe and a wooden rake. A late 18th-century traveller listed a peasant's labours: he dug the ground with a mattock (a large pick with a blade set at right angles to the handle), drew the plough in place of a buffalo, distributed water, worked 'chain pumps' and lifted enormous burdens. And then there was the work on the terraces which

MATERIAL SUCCESS   Silkmakers reel their material in a factory. Soft, strong, light and hard-wearing, silk was a wonder fabric, luxurious and practical at the same time.

had to be laboriously carved out of the hillsides, with carefully constructed paths between them and the elaborate tracery of irrigation canals – all needing constant maintenance.

If the peasant's labours were hard, his rewards were few. Nearly two-thirds of his income went in tax, some of it payable in best-quality 'official rice' which was too valuable to eat at home. He was subject to all the catastrophes of floods, droughts and insect plagues which could wreck his livelihood and bring an inevitable train of famine and disease. In the Qing period something like half of all those born in China would die before they were ten years old. Even in good times, when the peasant got home there was little enough in the pot – an 18th-century writer commented that the Chinese man who had spent the day 'often in water up to his knees, in the evening . . . would think himself lucky to find rice, [and] cooked herbs [vegetables] with a little tea'.

ALL THE SILK IN CHINA

There were, of course, peasant families who were richer than the subsistence rice growers. Among them were those engaged in the cultivation of silk and tea.

Silk comes from the cocoons of silkworms which feed mainly on mulberry leaves. Once it was produced all over China – the Romans' name for China was Sericum related to the Latin *serica*, 'silk'. But by the Qing age it had become concentrated in a few favoured regions. In particular, it was a speciality of central coastal China – chiefly Jiangsu province and the northern part of Zhejiang province – where large areas were turned over to mulberry trees.

THE USES OF BAMBOO

Bamboo is one of China's most versatile resources, used for basket weaving, making rafts with built-in buoyancy and scaffolding. It is used for water pipes, fencing and tool handles. Bamboo tubes filled with gunpowder were used as rockets in battle and bamboo drilling-rigs were used to extract brine from underground deposits. They also piped up natural gas used to evaporate the brine to yield salt.

In these prosperous regions villages sprouted within a few hundred years into substantial towns and cities devoted to the range of activities associated with silk manufacture – for silk was never just one industry. At the edges of fields, trees needed to be cultivated and the silkworms fed; the cocoons had to be nurtured, and silk threads reeled from the cocoons – all tasks carried out by different specialists. Only then came the expert weaving of the delicate fabrics which had long made Chinese silks and satins famous the world over.

Rearing silkworms and reeling silk from the cocoons was a rural occupation, while weaving, too, was often the occupation of peasant households. However, the dazzling work needed for court costumes needed more elaborate methods. There were a number of imperial silk works, one of which, in the city of Suzhou in Jiangsu province, had 800 looms and more than 2000 workers in the early days of the Qing dynasty.

FERTILE TEA HARVESTS
Silk and tea were the most significant Chinese exports. In 1868 the two products made up no less than 94 per cent of the value of all China's export trade. Unknown in Europe before the middle of the 17th century, tea, in particular, had become Britain's national drink by the end of the 18th century when the British were drinking 30 million lb (14 million kg) of it each year. China was the world's only source until the 1830s when planters started cultivating tea in India using a previously wild strain from Assam. Despite such competition, China was still the world's leading exporter

in the mid-1880s, producing a total of 300 million lb (136 million kg) of tea in 1886 against India's 90 million lb (41 million kg).

Tea grew in many varieties and, like rice, imposed its own rhythms. The soil on the plantations had to be tilled and sown, and the shrubs pruned to stop them from growing into trees. The leaves had to be plucked and dried on the

DRESSED TO IMPRESS This silk robe, decorated with an imperial phoenix, belonged to the Empress Dowager Ci Xi. A silk merchant (below) shows off his wares.

out in small-scale family concerns – Chinese rural life was always a matter of farming the fields and engaging in handicrafts at home. Thus cotton – which in early and mid 19th-century America came from gigantic plantations with armies of slave labour and was turned into cloth in the great industrial towns of Lancashire – was in China a family business.

Similarly, sugar, the most infamous of the New World's slave industries with its teams of labourers in the canefields and insufferable conditions in the milling and refining compounds, was also in China a family business. The tall canes were cut, stacked and carted by the farmer himself, while travelling specialists turned it into sugar.

In the cotton and sugar industries, as in all the occupations of rural life (including farming), women were a vital element in the work force. George Staunton, secretary to Lord Macartney's embassy to China in 1793, noted: 'The wives of the peasantry are of material assistance to their families, in addition to the rearing of their children, and the care of their domestic concerns; for they carry on most of the trades which can be exercised within doors. Not only do they rear silkworms, and spin the cotton, which last is in general use for both sexes of the people; but the women are almost the sole weavers throughout the empire.'

VILLAGE LIVING

Rural life was focused on small villages, usually of only 200 to 400 inhabitants. They were clusters of brick or mud-brick dwellings whose families were probably linked by lineage ties. The village would have an ancestral hall for worshipping ancestors and a temple where festivals and ceremonies took place. There were more than a million such villages

TAKING TROUBLE WITH TEA
Workers in an 18th-century watercolour (above) pack tea for export to Europe. Another worker (left) waters tea bushes by hand.

same day, and then packed for transport. Tea sent overland, which included exports to Russia, was compressed into tea cakes; by water it went as leaf in crates.

Peasants grew it in the silk provinces of Zhejiang and Jiangsu, and it was also widely grown in more southerly Fujian (Fukien) and in remote Sichuan (Szechuan) and Yunnan. It brought prosperity to many regions that grew it, allowing their farmers higher standards of living than their counterparts in the rice regions.

FAMILY CONCERNS

Although cereals, silk and tea were the chief crops of Qing China, a great deal else was cultivated. Peasant products ranged from necessities like cotton for clothing to luxury fruits and vegetables to supply the cities. All such production was carried

ANOTHER CHINA: LIFE ON THE FRONTIER

FAR BEYOND THE CROWDED CITIES and well-tended countryside of the Chinese heartlands lay very different regions – the vast, wild frontier zones added to the territory of the empire by Manchu conquest and then populated by encouraging migration. Most of these lands lay in the west towards central Asia, but they also included Taiwan to the east and the Manchus' own northern homeland, Manchuria. The heartlands also saw peasants colonising new territory as population pressure drove them out of plains and river valleys into hills and mountains. At the same time, the spread of 'New World' crops like maize, potatoes and peanuts enabled them to cultivate soils unsuitable for rice or wheat.

Moving into virgin lands, the settlers practised a 'slash and burn' technique to clear fields for their crops and moved on again when yields began to fall. It was a total contrast to the painstaking attention to maintaining soil fertility in rice-growing areas. Immigrant farmers were scattered and mobile, usually living in hastily built hovels. Official documents often referred to them contemptuously as 'shed people'.

Development in Taiwan was concentrated on the coastal plains, separated from the mainland by 90 miles (145 km) of rough sea infested by pirates. Penetration of the interior was limited by high mountains and head-hunting native peoples. Rice and sugar cultivation, hunting huge herds of deer for their skins, antlers and meat and trade with Japan and the Philippines brought a measure of legitimate prosperity, while secret societies also flourished. The 100 000 Chinese of 1683 numbered almost a million a century later, though the largest city and port Tainan (Taiwanfu) still had fewer than 50 000 people.

The frontier offered not only free land but also rare plants and precious metals, which attracted both individual adventurers and organised gangs. Frontier populations tended, therefore, to be predominantly male and young.

Compared with old settled areas, frontier society was more ethnically diverse and more egalitarian – but also more militarised and violent. In 1735 Manchuria alone was reckoned to have 100 000 criminals banished there for life from China's core provinces. There were not only conflicts between Chinese and local nomads or hill-tribes but also fights over mines or forests and vendettas between migrants from different regions. There were even uprisings against the intrusion of the central government, as it tried to impose public order, establish garrisons and collect regular taxes.

The most effective civilising force was commerce as merchants settled in trading centres and began to sponsor such stabilising institutions as temples and schools. In the end, however, the Qing dynasty had only limited success in incorporating the frontier settlers into the larger society of China as a whole. In part this explained the upsurge of rebellions in peripheral areas in the 19th century. These were often spearheaded by religious cults, ethnic brotherhoods or plain outlaw gangs.

by the end of the Qing period. But community life was strictly limited in such small settlements. They could not even support shops and permanent markets. So 'periodic markets' developed and out of these grew market towns providing not only outlets for peasants with surplus goods to sell, but a form of social centre as well.

A periodic market was one that opened for only a few hours – perhaps three or four – a few days in the week. Not every village had one, but there was always one within reach, for a village with a periodic market also served the surrounding villages, generally five or six of them. It was rare for any peasant family to be more than 6 or 8 miles (10 or 13 km) from such a market. Typically, a market trader would set up his stall in one village with a periodic market and travel a circuit of neighbouring villages with markets on each of the following ten days. He would then return to his base for supplies – before beginning again. His circuit was made with other members of the travelling market to which he

ARID HIGHLANDS

China's densely populated river valleys coexist with vast regions which are virtually empty. Four-fifths of the country is mountainous, including one-fifth that is over 15 000 ft (4600 m) in altitude. An area the size of western Europe is high plateau, so arid that even nowadays the average population density there is one per sq mile (0.4 per km^2).

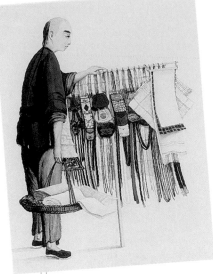

STREET SELLERS A pedlar (left) displays his stock of handkerchiefs on a stand. A pipe-smoking nurseryman (below) offers potted plants and miniature trees.

intermediate towns, in turn, formed links with central market towns, and so on through local cities to the regional capitals. As the markets ascended the scale, goods became increasingly specialised and exotic, since obviously the requirements and wealth of larger communities greatly exceeded the horizons of the humble peasant in his village.

A CRISIS OF TRANSPORT

These horizons were, despite the markets, severely restricted – not least because of the sheer difficulty of transport which created a semi-permanent crisis in Chinese life. Roads hardly existed, and those that did were little more than paths worn down by generations of use. They were scarred by potholes and wound tortuous routes around networks of fields. Sometimes they had eroded to a level 60 ft (18 m) or more beneath the surrounding land, especially in the north where the fine-grained clayey soil eroded easily.

Such paths twisted at the bottom of deep ravines, so narrow that usually only one cart could travel along them at a time. And the ravines became river torrents when it rained. Under such conditions, travelling a few miles was often a considerable achievement, while even the fastest packhorses could average only 30 miles (48 km) a day.

In fact, carts and packhorses were a rarer sight than the single peasant bent underneath a load that he carried across his shoulders using a pole. Or sometimes he would be pushing a larger load on a wheelbarrow. If the ground and wind were suitable he would fix a mat sail to a bamboo rod and create a 'ship on wheels'. Yet whatever he tried, land transport was hazardous, expensive and slow.

The state of the roads gave enormous advantages to the south which was interspersed with rivers, streams and canals. Small sampans on narrow streams carried up to 1600 lb (725 kg) and junks on larger rivers some 70 tons. Waterways were filled at all times with boats of every kind. Travelling one

belonged and its schedule was regular and known; other traders kept to their own circuits.

Market days found traders carrying their goods across their shoulders on poles or pushing carts and wheelbarrows to a temple courtyard or any other suitable site to lay out their products. With them came the characteristic one-man 'service industries' – barbers, scribes, doctors, 'tooth artists' (dentists), tool sharpeners, fortunetellers, even blacksmiths. Meanwhile, people from the surrounding villages brought chickens, ducks, surplus eggs, vegetables or homespun cloth – whatever they had to sell. So goods were bought and sold, and social life broadened at tea houses, food stores and wine shops.

These markets were, in fact, the first rung of a ladder. A group of them combined to serve a larger town with an 'intermediate market' where traders bought and sold in wholesale quantities. Groups of river, an awestruck John Barrow wrote: 'I firmly believe that all the floating vessels in the world besides, taken collectively, would not be equal either in number or tonnage to those of China.'

By the Qing period China's seamen had ceased the pioneering exploits which some hundreds of years earlier had taken them across the Indian Ocean to East Africa. Barrow wrote, with a hint of sarcasm: 'The present system of Chinese navigation is to keep as near the shore as possible.' But just as he was struck by the sheer volume of shipping, so he was impressed by the good humour of coastal and riverside dwellers where 'on board the yachts constant mirth and good humour prevailed among the seamen'. He recorded how, as the sailors pulled on the massive oars – six to ten of them per oar – 'they sang a sea song intoned by the master and taken up as a chorus by the rowers, to lighten their labour and assist in keeping time with the strokes'.

The river was, indeed, its own community, for there were 'floating villages' with 'more than 600 large vessels, each having a range of ten or twelve distinct apartments built upon the deck, and every apartment contained a whole family'. Barrow reckoned that 'in the distance of 90 miles [145 km] on [one] small branch of a river, there were floating on the water not fewer than 100 000 souls'.

Villagers of China's coasts, waterways and lakes earned their livings as fishermen and carriers. No visitor left without stories of life in the fishing villages – how the women assisted in hauling the nets, and how those who lived on boats towed along bamboo rafts as 'floating gardens' where they grew onions and garlic to supplement their fish diets. And, always, there were the tales of the cormorants, 'the famed fishing bird of China . . .

NO HIGHWAY Packhorses tramp along a characteristically rutted road through a mountain pass only 25 miles (40 km) north of Beijing.

EYEWITNESS

'TAKING BREAD OUT OF STONE'

THE SCOTTISH PHOTOGRAPHER John Thomson, travelling by boat through the gorges of the upper Chang Jiang (River Yangtze) in 1871, noted the primitive homes of the local people but was impressed by their 'frugality and industry':

❝ Rude fisher-huts, perched here and there upon the lofty cliffs, afford the only evidence of the presence of man. A few miles further on we came upon several houses of a better class, surrounded by patches of orchard ground. The inhabitants here obtain a livelihood by selling the produce of their gardens to the passing boats. To these more civilised dwellings there succeeded abodes of a most primitive type – cave hovels, closed in front with a bamboo partition, and fitted with doorways of the same material. These cabins were erected in the most inaccessible positions beneath overhanging cliffs, and their smoke-begrimed interiors reminded me of the ancient cave dwellings which sheltered our forefathers at Wemyss Bay in Scotland. It is in just such desolate spots as these that the frugality and industry of the Chinese race are most conspicuously exhibited. A number of the hardy natives live by fishing, while others are engaged in the stone-quarries close by; and whenever it is at all possible, the thin soil on the face of the rocks is scraped and planted, and vegetables, tended with ceaseless care, grow up there and mature. This is indeed taking bread out of stone. ❞

instructed in the art and practice of supplying its owner with fish in great abundance'. They astounded George Staunton: 'On each boat or raft are ten or a dozen birds, which, at a signal from the owner, plunge into the water; and it is astonishing to see the enormous size of fish with which they return, grasped within their bills. They appeared to be so well trained, that it did not require either ring or cord about their throats to prevent them from swallowing any portion of their prey, except what the master was pleased to return to them for encouragement or food.'

The waterways nourished the soil, too, periodically flooding the surrounding land and leaving behind rich mineral deposits. The plains and deltas of the Huang He (Yellow River) and the Chang Jiang (River Yangtze), in particular, had some of China's richest farmlands – as did the region lining

the monumental Grand Canal or Da Yunhe, the greatest inland navigation route in the world, linking Beijing with Hangzhou.

They impressed John Barrow once more as he looked along the canal at 'a most delightful part of the country, crowded with temples and villages and towns and cities'. Here the land was 'broken into hill and dale', and 'few of the detached houses or temples were without extensive gardens and orchards'. He saw fields of apples, pears, plums, peaches, apricots and pomegranates as well as enormous varieties of vegetables. It was the Chinese countryside at its most lush and fertile.

BULK CARRIER A junk lies at anchor around 1868. The Chinese invented the hinged stern-post rudder and watertight bulkheads to maintain buoyancy if the ship was damaged below the water line.

KEEPING THE EMPIRE AFLOAT

A SAMPAN is a floating home and farmyard for its owners. On the busy lower reaches of the larger Chinese rivers, families lived aboard the vessels which gave them their livelihood as hauliers, sharing their cramped quarters with livestock and poultry. In addition, the harbours of major ports housed whole floating villages of boat-dwellers.

In a mountainous country where travel by land was always slow and often dangerous, rivers and canals served as safe, comparatively swift highways. Large sums of state revenue were set aside for clearing and embanking watercourses and for constructing flood-control systems. Waterways were vital for transporting surplus grain from the empire's economic powerhouse, the warm, fertile south, to its political heart, the cold, dry north, near the barbarian frontier. They also provided the all-important irrigation which permitted double and even triple cropping.

HOME AND GARDEN

Chinese homes in both town and country were designed, above all, to be secure and practical.

Privacy was definitely valued over display. Surrounding walls provided suitably

modest shelter for the low buildings and courtyards within.

MOST CHINESE HOUSES were built around a courtyard. They were low and set directly on the ground with only the shallowest of 'foundations' to support a series of wooden pillars. These pillars in turn held the roof, which might be thatched or made of wood and tiles, depending on the region. The space between the pillars was filled in with wood or cob, a mixture of clay and straw. The Chinese phrase for a building translates literally as an 'enterprise of earth and wood', and these were the basic materials for houses, mansions, temples, public offices, army barracks and prisons throughout China.

Buildings of more than one storey, often with red-plastered outer walls, were a sign of opulence. In Beijing it was the palaces, the temples and the *yamens* (residences and offices of public officials) that had red walls – the yellow-glazed tiles of the Imperial Palace were also famous. The dwellings of ordinary people, by contrast, were a monotonous grey from the outside.

Beijing also had imposing terraces, steps and balustrades of white marble while the foundations of some of its palaces were of marble, too. But outside the Imperial City, stone of any kind was a rarity, usually reserved for bridges. The embassy under

COURTYARD COMMUNITY The cheerful chaos of this crowded scene reveals the courtyard as the focal centre of Chinese family life. Here the different generations work, relax, play or gossip.

'FULL OF SMOKE AND INTOLERABLE STENCH'

IN 1844 two French missionaries, Fathers Huc and Gabet, set out on a trek from China, across Mongolia to Tibet. The state of the inns in China's frontier regions provided a foretaste of the rigours to come. The *kang*, a heated brick platform, was the focus of such establishments:

❛ Inns . . . consist almost universally of a large square enclosure, formed by high poles interlaced with brushwood. In the centre of this enclosure is a mud house, never more than 10 ft [3 m] high. With the exception of a few wretched rooms at each extremity the entire structure consists of one large apartment, serving at once for cooking, eating and sleeping; thoroughly dirty, and full of smoke and intolerable stench. Into this pleasant place all travellers, without distinction, are ushered, the portion of space applied to their accommodation being a long, wide *Kang*, as it is called . . . about 4 ft [1.2 m] high, and the flat, smooth surface of which is covered with a reed mat, which the richer guests cover again with a travelling carpet of felt, or with furs. In front of it, three immense coppers set in glazed earth, serve for the preparation of the traveller's milk-broth. The openings by which these . . . boilers are heated communicate with the interior of the *Kang* so that its temperature is constantly maintained at a high level . . . The *Kang* . . . is, till evening, a stage full of animation, where the guests eat, drink, smoke, gamble, dispute, and fight: with nightfall, the refectory, tavern and gambling-house of the day is suddenly converted into a dormitory. Travellers who have any bedclothes unroll and arrange them; those who have none settle themselves as best they may in their clothes, and lie down, side by side. . . . When the guests are very numerous they arrange themselves in two circles, feet to feet. Thus reclined, those so disposed, sleep; others, awaiting sleep, smoke, drink tea and gossip. The effect of the scene, dimly illuminated by an imperfect wick floating on thick, dirty, stinking oil, usually in a broken tea-cup, is dream-like, and to the stranger, quite frightening. ❜

Lord Macartney dispatched by the British government in 1793 found that village houses in northern China consisted mostly of 'masses of earth baked imperfectly in the sun, or moulded between planks'. Alternatively, some homes were built 'of wickerwork, defended by a coating of clay'. Western travellers were surprised by the absence of historic architecture – there were few centuries-old temples, castles or palaces to commemorate China's past.

In fact, China's housing reflected a rural society with its own ancient traditions, which included an aversion to overt display. Laws restricting ostentatious buildings had a long history. Before the Qing period it had been forbidden for people outside the 'superior' classes to adorn their homes with the characteristic curved roofs, supported by brackets, of Chinese architecture. The custom persisted under the Qing dynasty, though then as before those who were wealthy enough could usually afford to ignore it. A similar attitude encouraged the construction of low buildings. Hidden, walled dwellings would lose their point if the houses soared above the walls.

At the same time, for people with enough land, the needs of ever-growing families spanning several generations were much easier to meet with a flexible network of linked one-storey apartments. The same basic plan of interconnected living quarters shielded by a surrounding wall was adopted by most Chinese families.

HOMES THAT FACED INWARDS

Grand or humble, all Chinese houses were designed to look inwards. Through the front door lay a courtyard, with apartments on each side. For the poor the courtyard was tiny, the rooms on each side primitive and, in the countryside, the small compound was probably shared with livestock. The courtyards of the better-off were naturally more extensive. They might spread into a whole interconnected 'village' with separate apartments including a dining room, a reception area and establishments for different family members, guests and servants. Windows were almost always covered with paper since glass was rare.

Sheltered from the public gaze, these courtyards and apartments might be lavishly ornamented in wealthy homes. *The Dream of the Red Chamber*, an 18th-century family saga and among the most popular books in Chinese literature, describes the heroine Daiyu entering the mansion of rich relatives for the

A Craze for Things Chinese

THE GREAT SKILLS of China's furniture-makers led to a fad in 18th-century Europe for 'Chinoiserie'. In 1703 a French ship, the *Amphrite*, sailed from Nanjing (Nanking) with a cargo consisting entirely of Chinese lacquer-work. It marked the beginning of a craze and by the middle of the century European salons decorated with Chinese wall-papers and silks were being filled with Chinese cabinets, tables and screens, while blue-and-white porcelain was displayed on the dressers of humbler homes.

European craftsmen also began to adopt Chinese subjects and motifs. In about 1734 the English cabinet-maker William Lennell made a 'Chinese' bed for the stately home Badminton House, and for a time mahogany pieces of all kinds became 'Chinese' by including fret-work, a temple roof or a pagoda or two. At the same time European craftsmen were mastering the Chinese arts of inlay and carving.

COLLECTOR'S DELIGHT Miniature Chinese wares like this porcelain pagoda were highly attractive to European connoisseurs with a penchant for the exotic.

Chinese lacquer, meanwhile, was making similar conquests. It is the processed sap of a shrub-like tree, *Rhus vernicifera*, native to southern and western China. The sap, when refined of impurities by straining and heating, can be coloured and applied to most surfaces, usually pinewood or hemp-cloth, but also metal, porcelain and basketwork. The coating is durable, imperme-able, heat-resistant and makes the item it coats resistant to attack by insects. The coating of lacquer is applied in successive thin layers, sometimes as many as 200, each of which must be dried in a damp, dust-free

atmosphere for several days. The final layer can be polished or decorated by paint-ing, incising, inlaying or carving.

Originally lacquer was valued as a preser-vative for timber used in buildings and on wooden food vessels. It fell out of fashion with the inven-tion of porcelain under the Tang dynasty (AD 618-906) and did not regain popularity until the Ming period (1368-1644), when it was used purely for decorative effect.

By the 18th century lacquerware was being used almost exclusively for ornaments and collected by con-noisseurs. The craftsman's mastery of the technique was reflected in the weight of dozens of layers of different-coloured lacquers, deeply incised to achieve decorative effects with contrasting hues depicting flowers, birds, animals or even whole landscapes. Most lacquered goods were small, such as dishes, bowls and trays, but large items such as screens, chests and writing-boxes, inlaid with gold, silver, jade, ivory, coral or mother-of-pearl, were produced under imperial patronage. They came from a factory founded within the imperial palace at Beijing by the Kangxi Emperor in 1680.

During the same period lac-quered and inlaid furniture was exported to Europe, many items selling on their novelty rather than their quality. Quite often decorated panels were sold on in bulk and cut up by European craftsmen to be refashioned into items totally unknown to the Chinese, such as picture frames.

CABINET OF CURIOSITIES Lacquer cabinets had drawers and secret compartments where their owners could house prized coins, curios and other such collectables.

first time: 'Each hand resting on the outstretched hand of an elderly attendant, Daiyu passed through the ornamental gate into a courtyard which had balustraded loggias running along its sides and a covered passageway through the centre. The foreground of the courtyard beyond was partially hidden by a screen of polished marble set in an elaborate red sandalwood frame. Passing round the screen and through a small reception hall beyond it, they entered the large courtyard of the mansion's principal apartments. These were housed in an imposing five-frame building resplendent with carved and painted beams and rafters which faced them across the courtyard. Running along either side of the courtyard were galleries hung with cages containing a variety of different-coloured parrots, cockatoos, white-eyes, and other birds.'

BARE AND COMFORTLESS
Such a mansion was, of course, exceptional. The interiors of Chinese homes more often struck Western travellers as bare and comfortless. The diplomat Sir John Barrow, a member of Lord Macartney's mission, described the houses of the peasantry: 'Four mud walls covered over with a thatch of reeds, or the straw of millet, . . . compose their

habitations; and they are most commonly surrounded with clay walls, or with a fence . . . A partition of matting divides the hovel into two apartments; each of which has a small opening in the wall to admit the air and light; but one door generally serves as an entrance, the closure of which is frequently nothing more than a strong mat.'

Other Western observations were downright critical. 'There is not a water closet in all China' was one practical complaint. Besides observing that the Chinese were 'ill-washed', Lord Macartney observed with distaste: 'They seldom have recourse to pocket handkerchiefs, but spit about the rooms without mercy, blow their noses in their fingers,

BARE ESSENTIALS These beggars in Fuzhou (Foochow) have made their home among the dead, special chambers where bodies were stored until ready for burial. Even the residence of a gentleman (left), seen here playing with his children, is only sparsely furnished.

77

TRADITIONAL TASTE Symmetrically placed furniture, calligraphy and miniature trees adorn this room of around 1850.

wipe them with their sleeves, or upon anything near them. This practice is universal and, what is still more abominable, I one day observed a Tatar [a Manchu] of distinction call his servant to hunt in his neck for a louse that was troublesome to him.'

The lack of privacy in Chinese homes also struck observers. In more affluent houses wood and paper screens or cloth curtains sufficed to separate the rooms from each other, although these and other features were often richly adorned. The doorways

OYSTER-SHELL WINDOWS

Oyster shells were used in some parts of China as a substitute for glass. The shells were carefully scraped until they were so thin they became semitransparent. They were then set into small square frames and a number of these oyster-shell panes were fitted into a window.

The elaborate 'dragon robe' worn by emperors and high officials might take 12 workers as long as five years to embroider.

were decorated, sometimes with paintings but more often with written scrolls quoting a homily or the work of a famous sage. The wooden beams were sometimes decorated, too, carved or painted with images of fruit, flowers and birds.

Wooden or lacquerware pillows attracted further Western criticism. The Chinese pillow 'is not', wrote one traveller, 'intended to be something soft and comfortable on which to recline the head but simply as a rest for the neck. It consists of a variety of articles according to the financial position of the individual. With the very poor it is a block of wood or a brick. This is placed under the nape of the neck . . . The richer have more elaborate and expensive ones, but always of some hard and unyielding substance.'

Furniture was comparatively sparse even in rich homes, but the items that existed were often superbly crafted. They consisted mostly of dark-wood chests and cabinets for storage and, in the south, large curtained beds. Country people did much of their work in the fields sitting on tiny, low stools and these they also used in the home. In southern China, small, low bamboo chairs were used by the poor, as well as narrow benches for eating at table.

Richer people had high, hard chairs and tables made of polished wood.

In the north, living rooms had a raised platform called a *kang*. It was usually about 2 ft (60 cm) high, made of stone or brick and heated by interior piping in winter. It was covered with mats and cushions and low tables. Here people slept in winter and received friends, sharing tea and wine crosslegged. The *kang* took up most of the space in the room.

No one except a close relative or friend would take off his shoes and go up to the *kang* unless invited. In *The Dream of the Red Chamber*, Daiyu is reluctant to do so even when her aunt invites her.

ALL TOGETHER Families valued privacy from the prying eyes of neighbours, but within the home there was no such thing. In poor homes, eating, sleeping and working took place within a few feet of each other.

Not surprisingly the *kang* in her relatives' home is covered with a scarlet Kashmir rug and sumptuously furnished: 'In the middle of the *kang* was a dark-red bolster with a pattern of medallions in the form of tiny dragons, and a long russet-green seating strip in the same pattern.'

HOW TO DRESS CORRECTLY

As a rule, the Qing emperors allowed themselves to be moulded by the land they had conquered and supported most of its customs and ways of organising things with the full force of their law.

continued on page 82

COURTLY DRESS

People were what they wore in imperial China,

their costume proclaiming their rank in society.

ONE WESTERN TRAVELLER, Thomas Taylor Meadows, writing in the 1840s, had an acute eye for many of the finer points of Chinese clothing: 'Chinese dress . . . is generally supposed to be quite unchangeable . . . Now it is true that the Chinese always wear long gowns when they go out, just as we wear coats; but as every part of our coats and our other garments are constantly subjected to all kinds of changes, within certain limits, so the length of the Chinese gown, the size and form of its sleeves, its colour, and the kind of flowers worked in it when of silk . . . are perpetually varying.'

The most characteristic official garments of the Qing period included, for men and women alike, the *chaofu* and the *pufu*. The *chaofu*, the most Manchu of these garments, was a long robe, jacket-like on the top but turning into a full pleated skirt below the waist. It was worn for formal court functions and was also used as a ceremonial burial robe by state officials and their wives. By the end of the 19th century, when dress regulations were relaxed, lower-rank courtiers sometimes wore the pleated skirt separately over their ordinary coats to save the expense of buying a one-piece *chaofu*. The

ROBES OF OFFICE An 18th-century watercolour shows a high-ranking lady (above, left). A government official (above, right) wears a plain, dark *pufu* over the longer, more decorative *chaofu*.

tight lower sleeves differed in both colour and the materials used from the upper sleeves. The *chaofu* was, of course, embroidered and made of fine silk.

Another robe, the long *pao*, was full-length and belted, and it was worn by a far wider range of officials. It was often called a 'dragon robe' because of its highly fanciful decorative motif. Like the *chaofu*, it was made of silk.

The *pufu* was a plain, dark, unbelted surcoat. It was designed to be worn over other robes. It was on their surcoats that mandarins displayed their badges of office, special emblems that distinguished the nine ranks of civil mandarins and the nine corresponding ranks of the military. Ladies' surcoats, too, carried the various insignia of

SPLENDOUR BY DESIGN The ornate robes worn by the highest officials required hundreds of hours of highly skilled, painstaking labour to produce. Even the choice of colours and designs was rich in symbolism.

SUMMER STYLE The Empress Dowager Ci Xi is surrounded by eunuchs and dressed for a tour of her palace gardens. This summer robe (right), worn by a eunuch, bears the imperial dragon.

their husbands' rank including elaborately woven pheasants, peacocks, egrets, unicorns, tigers, bears and orioles according to grade.

Ranks were also distinguished by buttons of different precious stones worn on officials' caps and by different feathers also worn in their caps. Headgear was, indeed, as tightly regulated as the rest of the costume. Mandarins wore caps or bonnets with stiff perpendicular streamers projecting at the back; alternatively, they might wear tall conical hats. Women rarely wore hats but shaped their hair into elaborate coiffures incorporating

jewellery, bands, pins and flowers.

Qing robes of office were gorgeously embroidered in an array of colours. The craft reached its peak in the 18th century when the full-length gown or long *pao*, in particular, was designed to represent nothing less than a diagram of the universe. Embroidered bands and billows across

the lower part of the robe merged into fantastic designs of prism-shaped rocks, cloud formations and twisting dragons.

The colours, various shades of yellow for earth, blues and greens for wood, red for fire, white for metal, and black for water, reflected the five elements of Chinese philosophy. Images such as the crimson phoenix and white tiger combined with the rest of the designs to make startling effects.

FITTING FOOTWEAR Manchu men wore boots (right). Manchu women, who did not bind their feet, had platform soles (far right). The sharp pointed toes of the tiny bootees (far right, below) highlight the deformation caused by foot-binding.

There were, however, a few areas in which they left their mark. This was particularly evident in the personal appearance of rulers and ruled. Here 'dress and queue' rules introduced by the Qing brought about a drastic change. According to these, all males were compelled to shave the tops of their heads as a sign of submission, leaving only the hair growing from the back of the crown. Tens of thousands of Chinese were massacred in the first few decades of the regime for refusing to submit to this humiliation. By the 1690s, however, such dissension had become a thing of the past and the barber's trade flourished as never before. The hair left growing on the crown was never cut.

Dress codes were rigidly imposed, especially on officials. They were reinforced in 1759 by the Qianlong Emperor in a work entitled the *Illustrated Catalogue of Ritual Paraphernalia*. In a preface to it, the emperor gave a clear warning that, when it came to dress, the Qing were not going to make the mistakes of previous dynasties and abandon their own traditions in favour of those of the Chinese: 'We, accordingly, have followed the old traditions of our dynasty, and have not dared to change them fearing that later men would hold us responsible for this, and criticise us regarding the robes and hats; and thus we would offend our ancestors. This we certainly should not do. . . .'

The emperor's dress code applied to all sectors of society. It defined the materials permitted to each rank and graded costumes in richness, descending from the finest silks and satins allowed to the higher mandarins down to the cruder clothes worn by craftsmen, merchants and peasants. It also introduced new styles, and replaced the long voluminous robes and upturned slippers of the preceding ages with boots, trousers and more functional coats with narrower sleeves.

These changes were not, in fact, as revolutionary as they appeared. Even before the Manchus conquered China – when they were still a wandering people of the steppes – they had absorbed many elements of Chinese dress. The change was nonetheless an indication of new authority. The Manchus were a race of warriors and mounted archers, a history reflected in their costumes. Shorter coats with apron-like attachments, belts and splits or vents at the bottom were legacies of horsemanship. So too were leggings, tightly fitting necklines and cuffs, all protection against cold and wind.

THE GARDENER'S ART

The Qing left their mark on Chinese dress, but the Chinese garden continued sublimely true to its age-old traditions. The ideal of living in harmony with nature was central to ancient Chinese beliefs, and the Buddhist doctrine of reincarnation fostered a sense of community with animals and birds. This was reflected in the superb works of Chinese painters of plant and animal life. Domestically it was revealed in the intimate connection between homes and gardens.

The vast range of China's climate and soils ensured a plant life of astonishing diversity. Yet

PRACTICAL PURPOSES
The peasant's straw cloak (far left) kept off the worst of wind and rain and provided padding for his shoulders. Children's clothes (left) differed little from those of adults.

only a small proportion of native plants were cultivated in Chinese gardens. This was partly due to conservatism of taste but more specifically to the Chinese habit of regarding plants as symbols of ideas, moral qualities and emotional states. As the Qianlong Emperor expressed it in the 18th century: 'When I find pleasure in orchids I love uprightness; when I see pines and bamboos I think of virtue; when I stand beside limpid brooks I value honesty; when I see weeds I despise dishonesty.'

Sign of Shame **The shaven crown was decreed for Chinese males by their Manchu conquerors. The hair at the back was plaited into a pigtail or queue which sometimes reached knee-length.**

Many plants which excited European collectors in the 18th and 19th centuries were not considered as garden flowers at all by the Chinese. Indeed, flowers were never dominant in Chinese gardens; those that were grown were cultivated in single varieties to be appreciated one by one in their due season. They included peonies, roses, hydrangeas, hibiscus, camellias and chrysanthemums, all planted in pots or raised beds.

Chinese gardens were very different from most of their European counterparts. Instead of symmetrical paths on levelled ground, they were full of winding tracks, willow trees, pines and bamboo clumps, planted as if by chance. Steep gullies furrowed the sides of hillocks, their sides uneven with rocks. In all this, the aim of the gardener was to imitate the beauties and follow the irregularities of nature. A Jesuit missionary, Jean-Denis Attiret, writing of the famous public gardens of Yuan Ming Yuan, north-west of Beijing, described the underlying design as 'a beautiful disorder and a wandering as far as possible from all the Rules of Art'.

Artifice was definitely involved, however. Chinese gardeners achieved their effects by raising artificial hills and the careful grouping and sculpting of rocky outcrops. They also created artificial waterfalls, lakes and ponds where gold and silver fish darted to and fro beneath the floating water lilies. According to Confucius: 'Wise men find pleasure in water and the virtuous find pleasure in mountains.' The Chinese word for 'landscape' translates literally as 'mountains-and-water', and the aim of the

EYEWITNESS

Prince Gong: Dressed to Impress

When the British doctor D.F. Rennie met Prince Gong, the leading Chinese diplomat of his day, in 1861, he was sufficiently impressed to record his dress in minute detail:

❛ On the right thumb he wore a large and broad jade-stone ring, of a white colour, with an upper surface of reddish-brown . . . His dress consisted of a fur robe of the sea otter skin, over a purple silk dress, trimmed with ermine cuffs. His hat was of the ordinary Tatar [Manchu] kind, the turned-up portion being lined with black velvet. The hat was surmounted by a crimson silk knob . . . The Prince had two chains round his neck, one of amber-coloured beads, the other of large beads of red coral. Each of the chains had an appendage, with precious stones attached . . . Black satin boots completed his costume. ❜

The Man Himself **Prince Gong poses for the camera around 1872, when as Prince Adviser he was at the height of his influence.**

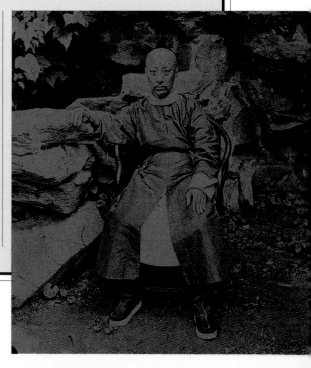

landscape gardener was to create a landscape in miniature. Here, the imagination might wander freely, withdrawing from the troubles of the world to contemplate the beauties of nature. Hence the pavilions that were carefully sited to provide vantage points and the open halls that were constructed for scholars to sit and seek inspiration as they wrote poetry or played musical instruments.

A PLACE FOR GOSSIP AND CONTEMPLATION

Contemplation, literary endeavour and social entertainments were considered suitable garden pastimes at all levels of society. In the 18th century an impoverished scholar, Shen Fu, described how he and his wife delayed their departure from a tiny cottage surrounded by fields in the suburbs of Suzhou – they had spent the summer there. 'I had asked our neighbour to buy us some chrysanthemums and plant them along the bamboo ledge. When the plants began to bloom, in the ninth month, [we] decided to stay for another ten days or so to enjoy their beauty and to send for my mother to come and see them also. The invitation pleased my mother and after she arrived we spent the whole day in front of the flowers, eating crab legs and gossiping.'

Of course, not every Chinese family could afford an elaborate garden, but flowers were cultivated in the most basic compounds. Herbaceous plants and dwarf trees were often grown in pots and displayed in courtyards, on terraces and on either side of the entrance to a home. Houses without gardens would grow lotus plants in their courtyards in large bowls filled with mud and topped up with water. And for every social class, the temple gardens, especially in Beijing and other cities, were favourite recreation grounds.

GARDENS OF DELIGHT Open-sided corridors blurred the distinction between inside and outside in the summer palace at Yuan Ming Yuan. This flower arrangement (right) conceals sophisticated conventions governing the choice of different types of plant.

85

EATING AND DRINKING

At its finest Chinese food was an art form, but only the wealthy could afford such fare.

Even for the poor, however, each region had its different traditions, generally speaking

spicier in the south and fishier in the coastal and wetland regions.

THE 18TH-CENTURY scholar and gourmet Yuan Mei was one of the most astringent of Chinese food critics. He was also a demanding guest to entertain, unimpressed by rank when it came to the all-consuming business of food: 'I was once asked to a party given by a certain Governor, who gave us plain boiled swallow's nest [regarded as a delicacy], served in enormous vases, like flower pots. It was utterly tasteless. The other guests were grovelling in their praise of it. But I said: "We are

FAST FOOD   These Chang Jiang (Yangtze) river folk were photographed tucking into their breakfast in 1871.

A PROVINCIAL CATERER – SETTING STANDARDS

YAO WAS AN EARLY RISER, from both habit and conviction. The habit came from years as a kitchen boy and under-chef in the residence occupied by a succession of gastronomically demanding magistrates – they had looked on food as a solace for exile in a provincial backwater. The conviction came from Yao's firm belief that the best meals come from the best ingredients – which meant being first at the market.

Striding between the stalls, with a sleepy-eyed kitchen porter shuffling behind him, Yao relished the deference he inspired as a customer of consequence. Sniffing, pinching, stroking and poking, he selected his ingredients and returned to his kitchen eager for work. Contemptuous of variety for its own sake, Yao had built his reputation and business on a limited range of classic dishes, such as trotters in vinegar or steamed fish in crab sauce. Today's offerings, the products of his dawn foray, would be goose feet, venison strips and deer tail. His menu always included some cheaper items

as well, like soup with chicken skin, because he consciously catered for all pockets, if not for all tastes.

As usual before setting to work, Yao spot-checked the entire range of kitchen utensils. His assistants knew that sloppiness was the surest way to earn his wrath, so he rarely found a blunt knife, grimy pestle or greasy chopping board. With a local shrine festival and a moon-viewing less than a week away Yao was hoping for good business from visitors from the surrounding villages. Summoning his eldest son to his side, Yao handed him the deer tails and venison strips and instructed him not to make a mess of them.

Never one to miss an opportunity, Yao set himself the no less exacting, and potentially as profitable, task of recycling yesterday's leftovers with slivers of salted duck and scallions (a kind of onion). This would make a cheap but tasty dish his second son could sell from a wayside stall near the temple gate.

The rest of Yao's day was all mapped out. After the lunch-time

rush he would take a siesta and then chat with cronies in the garden teahouse for an hour of calm. Then he would face the long and busy evening with its ever-nagging fear of having to tell a valued customer that, well, sadly, there was no more of what he wanted left but he could recommend . . .

FARM FRESH The humid climate of southern China in particular meant that many foods had to be bought daily. Others were smoked, dried or pickled and then stored.

here to savour swallow's nest, not to take delivery of it wholesale." If our host was just out to impress us he would have been better off to put 100 pearls in everyone's bowl. Then we would have known that

HEARTH IS HOME Fire-crackers are let off in honour of the Kitchen God. Of all the rooms in the home, only the kitchen had its own presiding deity.

the meal had cost him a fortune, without being expected to eat the uneatable.'

The rich and powerful could indulge such fine discriminations of the palate – and China did boast one of the most food-conscious of civilisations – but for most people food was a matter of subsistence. It was based on wheat (made into noodles, dumplings, steamed breads or pancakes) in the north and rice in the south. Periodic famines and years of shortage, sometimes leading to desperate uprisings, were a nagging fact of life, proof that many lived on or close

continued on page 90

DIET AND MEDICINE

A sound and varied diet was believed to be essential

for good health and sexual energy.

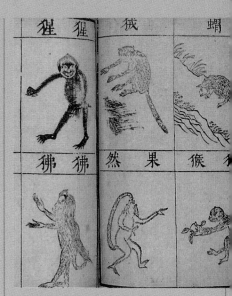

FOR THE CHINESE, a person was self-evidently what he or she ate. They believed that the internal 'balance' of the body was profoundly affected by one's food and drink. The system of the ancient Greek physicians Hippocrates and Galen, which stated that the body consisted of four 'humours' (wet, dry, hot, cold), was taken over by the Chinese, via the Middle East, in Han times – lasting until the 3rd century AD. They then reformulated it to fit their existing *yin-yang* concept of balancing opposites.

WELL-STOCKED MIND A scholar enjoys the varied scents of a herb garden. Knowledge of the healing properties of herbs and other plants showed that a gentleman was well-read and well-travelled.

In traditional Chinese theory, foods were primarily classified on a heating-cooling spectrum. Heat was gauged by its effect on the body, rather than its temperature. Heating foods were spicy, high in calories, subjected to high temperatures in cooking and rich in flavour. Eaten to excess they were believed to cause symptoms classified as 'hot' or 'tight' or 'red' – rashes, sores, fevers or constipation. Cooling foods were low in calories and bland in flavour, such as watercress or white radish. But even these, taken immoderately, were believed to cause upsets such as pallor, shivering or lethargy.

A wide range of foods, including the staple grains and various kinds of fish, fruits and vegetables, were

CATALOGUE This 1691 compilation records the medical value of all things edible, including six types of ape or monkey which it classifies according to their medical use.

regarded as being more or less around the midpoint on this scale and therefore broadly neutral in their effects. Their impact on the body could, however, be altered by the way in which they were cooked

basis might well regard dietary knowledge as an essential part of their professional expertise. Scholar-officials often dabbled in medicine – diet and medicine were, of course, seen to be closely linked – since it was one of the few fields of practical study which did not compromise their gentlemanly status.

Plants believed to be of medicinal value, such as ginseng, were grown on a commercial scale. Their cultivation was often encouraged by local officials. County gazetteers listing natural resources often had a category for medicinal herbs and roots. The immense manual of medicinal plants and animals compiled by the scholar Li Shizhen from 1552 to 1578 contained notes on nearly 1000 plants and 1000 animals.

EXPERIENCE AND EXPERTISE A 'street doctor' (above) treats a patient. The bronze doll (right) was used to teach acupuncture. It was covered with wax and when the pins were correctly inserted in the proper place water spurted out in confirmation.

CURE ALL? The root ginseng was among the most expensive of luxuries, once valued only against gold. It was believed to be a cure for most ailments and a recipe for long life. Ginseng, coming from the herb *Panax schinseng*, does have soothing qualities, but modern science has failed to confirm any of its other supposed properties.

– for example, by being baked or prepared using some other especially 'heating' method.

The basic hot-cool principle was refined by further categories of wet-dry and poisonous-cleansing. It was recognised that some foods, not normally toxic in themselves, could be for particular individuals or when eaten in combination with other foods. It was also realised that both a dirty cook and impure cooking water could foul otherwise excellent ingredients. The physical characteristics of foods were another factor that affected their evaluation. Red items were thought to be good for enriching the blood. Walnuts, resembling the brain, were thought to enhance its powers.

Modern science confirms that malnutrition diminishes the libido, and the link between physical and sexual energy was already clearly understood by the Chinese. So, many items labelled 'aphrodisiac' by Western observers of Chinese eating habits, were in fact simply high-protein elements esteemed for their general tonic and nutritional value. The inclusion of such dishes in banquets was regarded as highly desirable on both business and other formal occasions, such as weddings, birthdays or festivals – they were signs of the high status and good health of the person giving the feast. Similarly, sacrifices to the gods, especially at auspicious times such as New Year, customarily included much meat and brightly coloured fruit.

Although these beliefs were widely held, they were not necessarily held with equal intensity. Physicians, pharmacists and people involved in the growing, processing or selling of food on a commercial

SURROUNDED BY SQUALOR
The space outside the hut of
these Guangzhou (Canton)
slum-dwellers was their
kitchen. They even managed
to grow a few plants in pots.

a foot soldier 100. So a peasant needed to produce only a small surplus which, if he sold it, would take him above subsistence level – provided there was no natural calamity to destroy his crop.

Poor households throughout the Qing period spent about 70 per cent of their income on food, most of it cereals, only a small fraction, 1 or 2 per cent, on items like fruit. Poor but adequate would probably describe the diet of the majority in the 18th century, poor and inadequate in the 19th.

to the bread line. Such events were rarer in the 18th century, an age of relative prosperity, but became a marked feature of the unsettled 19th century.

In the long period of calm before the 19th-century troubles, the cost of most basic foods lay within the reach of many of the poor. The British emissary Lord Macartney recorded that, in 1793, 1 lb (450 g) of mutton or pork in Beijing cost 50 in the copper coins that constituted the everyday currency in China; 1 lb of rice 24; 1 lb of salt 35; a fowl 100, and a goose 500. He reckoned that a peasant could live on 50 cash a day, at a time when a boatman received 80 a day and

THE HONOURED GOURMET

Amongst the wealthy and educated, the gourmet had a distinguished ancestry. When Confucius was once asked a question about military tactics, he loftily declared that he knew all about the varying uses of a meat stand (*zu*) and a meat platter (*dou*) but had never troubled to learn about matters of warfare. Chinese literature is filled with specialist treatises on such subjects as turtle meat, lychees,

EYEWITNESS

THE DOUBTFUL PLEASURES OF WESTERN COOKING

THE BRITISH Doctor C. Toogood Downing was witness in the 1830s to one of the rare occasions when a high Chinese official was exposed to an offer of Western hospitality:
❡ Along the centre of the spacious apartment a table was placed, spread with a snow-white cloth and covered with dishes of the greatest delicacies in season. Blancmanges, jellies and fruits were abundantly

supplied, in addition to more substantial viands; and, in fact, everything necessary for a first-rate breakfast after the English fashion . . . The old man eyed the good things upon the table . . . and whispered to his attendants to fetch them for him. As each dish was brought successively, and held up to his eye, he examined it very carefully all around as an object of

great curiosity, and then languishingly shook his head, as a sign for it to be taken away . . . [He went on in this way] until he had looked at everything on the table, without finding a single article suitable to his delicate stomach . . . and when the table had been entirely ransacked, he shook his head once more in sign of disapproval, and then called for a cup of tea. ❡

CONSPICUOUS CONSUMPTION A convivial dinner party, served by numerous attendants, offered an ideal opportunity to show off one's wealth, taste and generosity. Women were never invited.

sea slugs and every other kind of delicacy. The 17th-century writer Li Yu confessed in a work on crabs that 'as far as crabs are concerned, my mind is addicted to them, my mouth enjoys the taste of them, and not a single day in my life have I ever forgotten about them'.

Moreover, the Chinese believed firmly in the links between healthy eating and a healthy body. Even their highest scholars, normally aloof from the more mundane areas of life, took pleasure in studying diet and medicine and would occasionally act as amateur doctors, diagnosing illnesses and prescribing complicated herbal concoctions.

The passion for food was perfectly compatible with the Chinese people's reputation for moderation. A favourite instruction from parents to their

PERFECT INGREDIENTS

The food authority Yuan Mei declared that the success of a fine banquet was only 60 per cent due to the chef. The rest of the credit belonged to the man who had bought the ingredients.

The scientific name for the peach is *Prunus persica* – Persian plum tree – but its true birthplace was ancient China, where it was believed to preserve the body in perpetuity and became a symbol for immortality. It reached Persia in the 3rd century BC and by the 1st century AD the Romans were importing it as the 'Persian apple'. At the court of Louis XIV the peach was known as 'Venus breast'.

children was that they should finish their meal feeling only 70 per cent full. At the same time, while banquets for the rich often included 40 or 100 or even several hundred dishes, many of these were provided simply to show the generosity of the host. Of the rest, the variety was there so that honoured guests could choose their particular favourites. In any event the food – eaten directly from communal bowls – was tasted rather than devoured. Those Chinese who could afford it sought a gastronomic and aesthetic experience rather than a European-style full belly.

Qing China recognised four main cuisines: northern, eastern (or Shandong), western (or Sichuan) and southern. Northern food tended to have strong, robust flavours, using plenty of garlic

STREET TREAT A child buys sweets from a street vendor. Nuts, dough and bean-paste were made into confectionery, often shaped like birds, animals or fish.

and spring onions. Southern food was blander, using a more delicate palette of flavours; a lot of steamed fish was also eaten in the south.

Eastern (Shandong) food was similar to southern but tended to be sweeter; it, too, included a lot of fish. The food of inland, western China was hot and spicy as in the north.

In all regions the basic principle of cooking was the same, for rich and poor alike. It was a principle of combination: most fundamentally, the combination of *fan*, that is cereal or starch, with 'dishes' or *cai*, prepared from meat, fish and vegetables. Poor

WHEAT, MILLET AND PIG'S MEAT: BEIJING PRICES

THE SURVIVAL of account books from the imperial court means that we can compare prices of what were presumably the top-quality foodstuffs on sale in the capital. Wheat was only slightly cheaper than rice, millet about 20 per cent cheaper than wheat. Pig's meat was so important that separate prices were quoted for a whole pig, for pork, trotters and liver sold by weight and for bladders and intestines sold by unit. A pig cost almost as much as two sheep but the intestines could be had for less than the price of two chicken's eggs.

A single goose cost more than four chickens, a duck the same as three chickens. Oranges, apples, peaches, pears, apricots and plums were evidently something of a treat, being sold singly, whereas grapes and cherries were sold by weight. Oranges were the most expensive fruit of all; the price of two oranges was equal to that of five peaches or more than 1 lb (0.5kg) of lychees.

Other foods on regular sale included fresh lotus roots and watermelon seeds. The purest honey cost 50 per cent more than sugar, which was the same price as edible seaweed. Ginger cost 50 per cent more when pickled than when fresh. The cheapest basic commodities were soya sauce, vinegar and bean curd.

households might well manage only *fan* with the occasional dish or *cai*.

The commonest *fan* included millet, rice, wheat, maize, yams and sweet potato. Soya beans, broad beans, peanuts, turnips, pork, dog, beef, chicken, duck, goose, pheasant and a range of fishes were some of the common *cai*. Ingredients included a few New World crops like sweet potato, maize and peanut that were imported into China only in the Qing period, rapidly becoming staples in the local diet. There were some areas during the 18th century in which maize and the sweet potato actually replaced rice as the main food of the poor.

COOKING FOR EXPERTS

The Chinese knew about every conceivable variety of edible plant, to the extent that we simply have no words, for example, for many of their 50 or so different kinds of bean. At the same time, however, their cooking was not focused solely on ingredients but also on the details of preparation, including the skills of slicing and chopping, assessing different food textures, the balance of flavourings and the effect of various combinations.

In preparing a meal, Chinese cooks always had to remember that the gentry and their wives for whom they worked were themselves accomplished gourmets. It was for the gentry, in fact, that food authorities and gourmets often wrote their learned dissertations. The quirky Yuan Mei was one such authority. He wrote for both cooks and fellow gourmets and always stressed the 'natural properties' of

WATER FLAVOUR Water birds were a source of protein and flavour, with feet and beaks regarded as particular delicacies. This bamboo raft was moored on the Ya river in Sichuan province.

RIOT! Economic crises in the 19th century brought food riots. Here starving peasants seize a cargo of grain.

every item of food. Pork had to be thin-skinned and fragrant; carp white of stomach and slender in shape; vinegar only expressed its 'true purpose' when it was sharp. Gristle had to be removed from the meat.

It was vital to achieve the right mix of blandness, clarity and richness in food combinations, and only fools would consider putting powdered crab with bird's nest or anything at all with such strongly flavoured dishes as eel, turtle or mutton. 'I always say,' noted Yuan Mei, 'that chicken, pork, fish and duck are the original geniuses of the board, each with a flavour of its own, each with its distinctive style; whereas sea slug and swallow's nest (despite their costliness) are commonplace fellows with no character – in fact mere hangers-on.'

All foods made their own demands on the cook. They needed their special kinds and degrees of heat and often different utensils. Clams, eggs, chicken and fish all had their appropriate cooking

temperatures, and cooks who kept peering into the pot merely invited the water to bubble too much and so lose the flavour. 'Certainly to have a fresh fish and to cause it to become unfresh is a terrible act', warned Yuan Mei. As for those who cooked

THE VERSATILE SWEET POTATO

When the sweet potato was first introduced into China from New World in the 17th century, it was valued as an emergency food that could be grown in times of drought. But it was soon found that it could be grown in soil too salty or sandy for grain, and eaten by young and old as well as scavengers, such as chickens, which were themselves edible. It could be boiled, ground and even fermented. Regardless of its humble standing in the hierarchy of desirability, its cultivation spread widely.

strongly flavoured foods in the same pot, the result was 'like chewing wax. I fear that these chickens, pigs, geese and ducks have souls and will lodge a formal complaint with the underworld'.

THE ETIQUETTE OF FOOD

There were dozens of foods associated with particular festivals or seasons. Dumplings were eaten at the New Year, moon cakes at the moon festival in mid autumn, while a sour prune drink and sweet melons were traditional summer fare. There were also some specific food offerings made to the deities and coarse foods eaten during periods of mourning.

Most regulated of all was the food eaten by the emperor, whatever his personal tastes might have been. A vast army of specialists worked in different departments devoted to meats, tea, pastries, wine, pickles, vegetables and hundreds more. The palace kitchens provided every rank in the imperial household with appropriate foods and utensils according to status. The emperor himself was served by processions of eunuchs carrying numerous dishes. At the end of the Qing era imperial records show that the emperor was being served 800 lb (360 kg) of meat and 240 chickens and ducks each month, even though the emperor concerned was the child Pu Yi. Not surprisingly, he did not get through it all and very often food was simply left to rot.

It was not only the emperor's food that was ordained by rule. There were six grades of Manchu banquet and five Chinese, given in appropriate styles and quantities to delegations that were visiting the emperor depending on their significance. Senior Mongol princes were served at the first Manchu level, the Dalai Lama at the fifth. Chief examiners for the civil service exams received the second Chinese grade, and the three top students the fifth. This graded approach was reflected in practices far beyond the palace. One group of merchants always divided their guest lists into those worth sixteen, ten or eight dishes. Their top grade included the famous delicacies bear's paws, deer tail, shark's fin, bird's nest and sea slugs, all eaten in soups. The second omitted bear's paw and deer tail, and sharks' fins disappeared from the third.

The right things to drink also had their vital part to play in feasting – especially the famous varieties of rice wine (similar to Japanese *sake*) that came from Shaoxing in the subtropical coastal province of Zhejiang. All Chinese 'wine' was, in fact, a spirit distilled from rice or millet. Sometimes fruits were added for taste, making quince, cherry or grape 'wine'. Flower petals, too, were used for their flavours.

Despite the Chinese people's reputation for abstemiousness, there were plenty of well-reported episodes of drunkenness among officials and others of the Qing period. The cookery writer Yuan Mei was quite open about his own escapades, admitting to drinking himself unconscious on his wedding night and on other occasions drinking to excess despite his best intentions to avoid such conduct. In his opinion, the rice wines from Shaoxing were vastly overrated

GOOD MANNERS Diners (above) contemplate their meal. Etiquette included niceties such as reversing one's chopsticks when dipping into a common plate. In the 1630s the Englishman Peter Mundy noted people's dexterity with chopsticks (right).

TEA: THE DRINK OF IMMORTALITY

CHINESE LEGEND attributes the invention of tea to the Shen Nong Emperor. He is supposed to have stopped on a hot day in 2734 BC to prepare a refreshing cup of boiling water. By chance he settled under a tea bush from which leaves fluttered down to make a refreshing drink whose aroma enthralled him as he raised it to his lips.

For centuries tea was valued by the Chinese as a tonic rather than a daily drink. In this they were not mistaken since it does aid digestion, stimulate the circulation and heart-beat, acts as a diuretic and is rich in manganese, iodine and copper.

As the best teas are cultivated 6560 ft (2000 m) above sea level, China's mountainous landscape provided a suitable environment. The Chinese developed dozens of varieties, with different places of origin, different flavourings added to them and different processes of drying or fermentation.

From China tea spread to Tibet, Mongolia, Korea and Japan. By the 13th century city teahouses had become popular social centres. The revolution that overthrew the Qing dynasty in 1911 was plotted in the back room of a Shanghai teahouse.

Tea was first brought to Europe in the 17th century; it reached Amsterdam in 1609 and England in 1644. The diarist Samuel Pepys recorded his first taste 'of tee, a China drink of which I never had drunk before' in September 1666; less than a year later he was drinking it at home. Initially Europeans drank it Chinese-style, without milk or sugar, from small bowls without handles. The leaves were so expensive that they were kept under lock

EXPORT MODEL This silver-gilt teapot was made for export to Europe around 1680. Chinese styles and motifs dominated the utensils Europeans used to drink tea.

and key in a special 'caddy' – which derives from the Chinese *catty*, a standard weight of 1⅓ lb (600 g).

From the 1720s onwards tea was imported direct to Europe from China rather than by way of Dutch-controlled Indonesia and tea-importing became a huge business. By 1808 the British were importing some 30 million lb (14 million kg) a year, more than twice as much as all the other importers put together. The Dutch and the Danes were also great tea drinkers (and smugglers of tea to heavily taxed Britain). The British introduced tea to Morocco, where, drunk very sweet with mint, it soon became the national drink.

TEA NAMES, TEA ROUTES

The names for tea in non-Chinese languages usually reflect the route by which tea first came to them. The English tea, French *thé* and Spanish *te* are derived from its name – *te* – in the dialect of the southern coastal province of Fujian (Fukien), from which it was exported by sea to western Europe. The Japanese *cha* and Russian *chai* and similar words in Persian, Turkish and Greek are based on *ch'a*, a north Chinese term. The English slang 'char', comes from the Hindi *cha*, which belongs with Japanese and Russian in the second group.

entertain their friends and acquaintances. The New Year was a particularly festive time – like our Christmas – when the well-to-do entertained and were entertained busily. Invitations to dinner, whether at home or in a restaurant, were sent out three days in advance. They were scrolls of long red paper with the name of the guest of honour heading the list; the others followed in order of precedence. A standard written form of acceptance was a phrase meaning that the guest would respectfully take the last seat, for of course the seating plan was an integral part of any occasion.

Rich people might have their breakfast at about 6 am, lunch at noon and dinner at about 6 pm – the poor could afford only two meals a day. But timing was never strict and dinner parties – always men-only affairs – often started very late because guests thought nothing of accepting several engagements

and he much preferred the stronger spirits that came from Fenjiu in Shanxi province and the *kao-liang* (a kind of millet) wine of Shandong.

Restaurants were fashionable throughout the Qing era and were where many people chose to

PICKED TO PERFECTION Harvesting tea (above) was a matter of fine judgment, and it had to be processed the same day. The Chinese recognised dozens of different varieties of tea plant (right).

on the same evening. Such banquets perhaps had more to do with giving or repaying favours than pure social friendship.

Nobody ate before the guest of honour had begun. It was customary for the host to raise his glass of warm wine and say '*qing*' ('please') as a signal for

THE ELEGANCE OF TEA The Duc de Conti, a French aristocrat, takes tea. Tea-drinking offered a stylish focus for group portraits on both sides of the English Channel in the 18th century.

the chief guest to help himself from the first of the dishes – the most important delicacies were served towards the beginning of the banquet. If a leading guest was unable to attend, his food would be sent to his home afterwards, and the same applied to favourite dishes missed when a guest was obliged to leave early. Senior officials brought bodyguards who had to be fed at the host's expense. The host also provided carriages and sedan chairs for those of his guests who did not have their own servants waiting for them.

THE CLASSIC ART OF TEA

Just as there were specialist cooks, so there were 'tea masters' whose wisdom was passed down through the ages. One was the Huizong Emperor who wrote a treatise on tea in 1107 in which he warned that 'teas vary as much in appearance as do

97

NOT THAT BAD — IF YOU HAVE TO EAT IT

ARCHIBALD COLQUHOUN, who made extensive journeys through China in the 1890s, found the food boring but not as awful as he had heard: ❛ . . . as stewed pork, roast pork, pork sausages and pig's-foot gelee are apt to pall upon the uncultivated Western palate, we were forced to enter a protest against the too frequent repetition of these Chinese dainties . . . We had a hard struggle with the cook, but he relaxed so far as to vary the pork menu with dried duck and salt eggs . . . Chinese food is by no means the horrible mess which Europeans generally believe it to be . . . The fixed impression in England is that puppy-dog, cat and rat, and so on, form articles of the daily menu. This, of course, is utterly absurd. A few of the very poorest class in Canton do eat them, it is true. The food of a poor family is usually rice, with a bowl of soup to wash it down; something salt and tasty as a condiment; pork, vegetables and macaroni . . . With the poorest people, rice and salt cabbage or salt fish, with a suspicion of pork only, is the daily ration. Our boatmen's food . . . often looked by no means bad; eleven hours' work would make me relish it, I am sure – though I confess that a trial did not prepossess me in its favour! ❜

the faces of men'. He detailed various methods for mixing hot water with powdered tea, and was especially complimentary about the flavour of white teas – unfermented teas coming from special plants with extra slender stalks and very thin, glossy leaves. The emperor also alerted his readers to the fact that steaming and firing the leaves needed considerable skill: if these jobs were not done correctly, the white tea 'will taste like ordinary tea'. Another connoisseur was Lu You, who wrote a famous treatise 'The Classic of Tea' in the 8th century AD. He was reputed to be able to distinguish the water from particular rivers and even the parts of the river the water came from.

By the time of the Qing dynasty, tea was firmly established as China's universal drink. The Manchus officially recognised tea as a necessity and exempted it from normal taxes. In the Manchu period the very best green teas were always expensive luxuries, though poor-quality black teas were cheap.

Naturally tea drinking was carried out according to its own formalities. In 1762 one European writer described how tea was drunk in a wealthy home: 'There are very suitable implements for that purpose, such as a decorated table, with a small stove beside it, boxes with drawers, bowls, cups, saucers, spoons for jam, [and] crystallised sugar in pieces shaped like nuts . . .' The sugar was held 'in the mouth whilst drinking the tea, for this has least effect on its [the tea's] good taste, and uses up less sugar. All this is accompanied by various preserves, both dry and liquid, the Chinese having a much better understanding of how to make them dainty and attractive than European confectioners.'

FAVOURITE COMBINATION A street-seller anticipates a common modern taste – beer with peanuts. Western-style brewing was introduced to China from Germany in late Qing times.

LAWS OF HEAVEN AND EARTH

For the Chinese, spiritual influences were all around them – in the forces of *yin* and

yang, the spirits of dead ancestors, the hierarchies of local and national gods.

Different religious traditions usually coexisted happily, although anti-foreign feeling

could give rise to posters like this – in which a judge orders patriots to slaughter the

Christian missionary pig and his sheep-like converts. Law and justice, meanwhile,

were administered according to a code that sought to anticipate every contingency.

SAGES AND SPIRITS

Just as the past was woven into the present, so the invisible world existed alongside what

could be seen and touched. The intellectual elite revered the heritage of ancient sages.

Others were more preoccupied with ghosts, spirits and gods.

CHINESE RELIGIOUS BELIEFS came from many different sources. Three thousand years ago, long before the Chinese people were united under the rule of a single emperor, they worshipped a variety of gods and ancestral spirits and had already evolved principles that would endure until the Qing period and beyond. Among them were the all-important principles of *yin* and *yang*. Nobody knows for sure how the theory arose but it was already well established by the time of China's most famous thinker Confucius (*c*.551-479 BC), and would continue to be a decisive influence on all areas of Chinese thought from medicine to the arts to the theory and practice of good government.

Yin-yang theory emphasised the importance of order, unity and harmony achieved through balance, and these were the great themes of all China's most influential thinkers. Among them Confucius stands pre-eminent. Works attributed to him and disciples such as Meng Zi (Mencius – *c*.371-289 BC) and Xun Zi (Hsün-Tzu – *c*.298-230 BC) shaped Chinese culture right into the 20th century. They exalted respect for ancestors, the duties of sons towards their parents and the importance of ritual. They also taught that loyalty and obedience were virtues to be offered to rulers who had themselves learned the 'way' of righteousness.

Sometimes the Confucians disagreed. Meng Zi, for example, taught the essential goodness of humankind while Xun Zi believed that people were innately evil and in need of education to teach them

WISE MAN Lao Zi's domed forehead suggests wisdom. But depicting him on a peasant's water buffalo implies that he was also remarkably approachable.

righteousness. Both men, however, emphasised the importance of study to increase one's moral awareness and encourage virtue, rather than the enforcing of a rigid law.

Another thinker was Confucius' contemporary Mo Zi (Mo Tzu), a reformer who attacked 'corrupt men with their elaborate showy rituals and music . . . [who] delude relatives with lengthy mournings and fabricated grief'. Mo Zi's followers, the Mohists, also stressed the importance of a supernatural world of ghosts. For them this spirit world had a direct bearing on people's lives in the material world. According to Mo Zi, disorder resulted when people 'are in doubt about whether ghosts and spirits exist and are not clear that ghosts and spirits are able to reward the worthy and punish the wicked'. Popular Chinese beliefs would cling to this notion well into the 20th century.

BACK TO NATURE

A further school of teaching was Taoism. Lao Zi (Lao Tzu) was a near-contemporary of Confucius but deeply scornful of him, preaching a doctrine opposed in every way to the ritualism valued by the Confucians.

In place of formality Lao Zi wanted spontaneity; in place of hierarchies he wanted a levelling in which nothing was or seemed to be more important than anything else. He wanted a return, as he saw it, to an ideal state of nature and a communion of the human spirit with trees, mountains and rivers. He rejected the emphasis the other thinkers placed on social order and duty, preaching instead

THE SAGE'S VASE The characteristic black cloth topknot marks out a Taoist sage on this four-sided vase. In the foreground is a miniature mountain landscape, believed to be a suitable theme for meditation.

the virtues of *wu wei*, the principle of not interfering with the natural order or pattern of things.

He wanted to achieve a state of mind in which even matters of life and death could be laughed at. Such a state could be known only through mystical experience; it could not be put into words. 'A Tao [Way] that can be told of is not a permanent Tao.' Learning was an enemy. 'Our life is limited,' he wrote, 'but knowledge is limitless. To pursue the limitless by means of the limited is dangerous.'

In its different way, Taoism's influence was as profound as Confucianism's. It is evident in China's traditions of contemplation and meditation and in the Chinese people's awareness of the power and beauty of nature. It also had a more down-to-earth, popular side – usually known as religious, as opposed to philosophical, Taoism – with hierarchies of priests who were experts in such fields as healing. Not surprisingly, this was the side that had the greatest appeal to most ordinary people. In times of sickness, they resorted to Taoist priests for magical potions made by writing a spell on a piece of paper, burning it and then making a broth from the ashes. While some Taoist priests were celibate and lived in monasteries, most were married with families and lived in towns and villages.

Taoist priests were also geomancers or diviners whose *fengshui* (literally, 'wind water') skills played a crucial role in daily life. It was they who divined

EYEWITNESS

WHAT THE MASTER SAID

CONFUCIUS' sayings, recorded in the *Analects*, emphasise the importance of humaneness:

❝ Sima Niu asked about humaneness. The Master said: "The humane person is hesitant in his speech." He said: "Hesitant in his speech! Is that all that is meant by humaneness?" The Master said: "To [be humane] is difficult, so in speaking about it can one avoid being hesitant?"

Sima Niu asked about the gentleman. The Master said: "The gentleman is neither worried nor afraid." He said: "Neither worried nor afraid! Is that all that is meant by the gentleman?" The Master said: "If when he looks within he is not diseased, then what does he worry about and what does he fear?" ...

LITERARY LEGACY Confucius was invariably depicted in the robes of a scholar. Here he also clutches an armful of scrolls recording his learning – to be preserved and passed on.

The Master said: "The gentleman is easy to serve but difficult to please. If in trying to please him one does not accord with the Way, he is not pleased. But when it comes to his employing others, he takes account of their capacity. The small man is difficult to serve but easy to please. Although one does not accord with the Way when trying to please him, he is pleased. But when it comes to his employing others, he seeks perfection in them." ...

The Master said: "Firmness, resoluteness, simplicity, and reticence are close to humaneness." ❞

the spirit influences bearing on construction sites and graves. Nobody would dream of burying a relative or starting a building project without consulting them to make sure of choosing the most auspicious site. The *fengshui* man's skills had to be particularly well-honed in the south whose hilly terrain deflected the lines of influence into complex patterns. The belief in *fengshui* was so great that near the end of the Qing period the development of railroads was seriously inhibited because it was believed that they would have a negative effect on the *fengshui* balance of the proposed routes.

SAINTLY SOLITUDE **Buddhist traditions of meditation, solitude and self-denial attracted adherents to remote mountains, such as Mount Wutai in Shanxi province.**

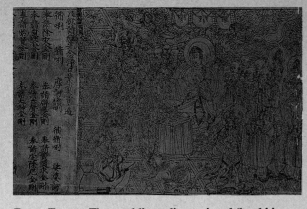

PRIME TRUTH The world's earliest printed 'book' is a 16 ft (5 m) scroll, the Buddhist Diamond Sutra, from AD 868. It is now housed in the British Library.

Buddhism, meanwhile, also made its mark on Chinese life. Originating in northern India about the time of Confucius, it became known in China possibly as early as the 1st century BC. With its teachings on reincarnation, it offered the Chinese a more clearly defined and comforting view of the afterlife than any of their other religious traditions. As a result, people usually asked Buddhist priests to conduct their relatives' funeral rites. The reverence Buddhism preached for all living creatures

PREACHING TO THE MULTITUDES

THE 19TH CENTURY saw large numbers of Protestant missionaries pouring into China. They never made large-scale conversions but did on occasion stir considerable interest. Here the English missionary Hudson Taylor describes an episode in the 1850s when he and a colleague named Edkins visited a lake island near the city of Jiaxing:

PATHFINDER Catholic priests and laymen of around 1860 kneel to pay their respects at the grave of an early convert in Macao. The first Christian missionaries to China were Catholics in the 16th century.

❝ Before we had finished looking round we observed a number of boats putting off in our direction, and soon a regular ferry was established between the island and the opposite suburb. The people came in multitudes, and those who could read were quickly supplied with tracts. When a large number had collected, Mr Edkins preached, and afterwards I had a long talk with some who gathered round me for books. By this time the numbers who had come were so great that we were obliged to go on board our boat, from which Mr Edkins again addressed the people . . .

As the crowd was continually receiving accessions, we thought it wiser to put off a little from the island, to prevent those who were behind from pushing the foremost into the water . . . Immediately, however, the people followed us, and in the middle of the lake we were surrounded by boats and kept hard at work supplying the newcomers with portions of Scripture and tracts. As fast as one boat was supplied it pushed off and another took its place . . . [What] joy it was . . . to think that not a few around us might shine forever like the stars of heaven in the Kingdom of our Lord. ❞

was another way in which it influenced Chinese life. There were regular days for 'the emancipation of animals' when people bought live fish in tanks in the local marketplace and released them into the surrounding rivers, and caged birds which they released into the skies.

Of course, there were, to the Western eye at least, a number of contradictions which observers occasionally pointed out – between, for instance, the Buddhist belief in reincarnation and the time-honoured Chinese practice of ancestor worship. But few Chinese concerned themselves with such apparent inconsistencies, even though foreign critics wondered how an ancestor could be worshipped who might already have returned to the world in another life.

A MEDLEY OF TRADITIONS

All these traditions – the age-old belief in spirits, Confucianism, Taoism and Buddhism – merged into and borrowed from each other and together created 'Chinese popular religion'. To the Chinese this religion was all around them – in the tablets dedicated to their ancestors at home, in family graves in the fields, in their villages and market-places just as much as in the shrines to local deities and the grander Taoist and Buddhist temples.

The spirit world was an essential part of this religion, and an ever-present reality for those who were still living. The Chinese took a decidedly practical view of the spirit world which bore a marked resemblance to the one they were familiar with, to the extent of being populated with spirit kings, magistrates and bureaucrats. It was to this spirit world that the souls of the dead made their first journey, initially to the awesome Ten Courts where they received judgment and suffered indescribable torments for 49 days. These courts, not unlike the boards that ran the various branches of the imperial government, were ruled by spirit officials who could be bribed. Thus sacrificial offerings of paper money eased the path of a dead relative by helping him to pay his way, as did rich food which kept him well nourished.

Other spirits and deities had more mundane, though no less vital, responsibilities. The most common was the Kitchen or Stove God whose job was to look after the household. Many families kept images of the Stove God in the kitchen. When a family split, departing younger brothers took hot

SERENITY AND SECRETS   A painting of 1663 (above), entitled Among Green Mountains I Build a House, evokes the tranquil lifestyle of a Taoist hermit. A porcelain pot for holding calligraphy brushes shows a Taoist wise man (left) sitting with some disciples.

coals from the old stove to guide the god to take up his place in the new home.

Earth gods also had an important part to play, each god holding responsibility for a particular village or group of villages. Peasants reported events

HEALING TOUCH A mother holds up her child so it can touch a temple statue believed to have healing powers. Touching the statue's eye was thought to bring healing to the eye, touching the ear to heal the ear and so on.

like births and marriages to their local earth gods and built shrines to them in their villages and fields and along pathways. The powers of these gods were confined to specific localities; if the peasant moved to a new district he worshipped a new earth god.

Above the local earth gods came a whole hierarchy of deities – once again reflecting the material world – that included city gods, gods of districts and gods of provinces. Among those at the top was the Jade Emperor, heavenly counterpart of the reigning emperor on Earth.

Most city gods were simply local heroes who had been deified. One was Qin Yubo, a prominent official under the Ming dynasty. After his death he was deified by the emperor – in a kind of posthumous ennoblement – and as a deity continued to look after Shanghai under the Qing dynasty. Such gods were believed to take an active interest in their cities' lives, helping to detect and punish crimes, and offering those who worshipped them protection from corrupt magistrates. Although they had started as ordinary mortals, an array of myths and legends soon grew up around them.

There were also thousands of gods with special powers. These included gate gods and bridge gods, gods for examinations, fish gods and insect gods, gods who were sages and healers. Many such deities were adopted from Buddhism, like the goddess Guanyin. As Avalokitesvara in India and elsewhere, 'she' was the male deity of compassion

GREATEST GIFT The bald God of Longevity is followed by an attendant bearing religious writings and a gourd full of medicine. The towering God of Wealth sports the long fingernails of a man of leisure. The God of Happiness offers the greatest gift – children.

and mercy but had become transformed in Chinese popular religion into a much-loved female deity believed to bring sons.

The heavenly realms also played their part in political life. The government was quick to identify with gods or spirits it regarded as bringing success, and bestowed honorific titles on them. In 1864, after the defeat of the Taiping rebellion in Nanjing (Nanking), the government gave the credit to the powers of the spirit world, proclaiming that the victory was entirely due to 'favoured protection from heaven and affection from the spirits of the sage ancestors'.

The traffic was not all one way. Gods were expected to perform and if they failed to do so they were discarded in favour of others. Or they might be dealt with in other ways. Western travellers were amazed at such sights as a magistrate solemnly

How to Fool the Phantoms

GHOSTS were believed in China to be ubiquitous, duplicitous and generally malevolent but, fortunately, not too bright. There were, therefore, a good number of tried and tested techniques for successfully deceiving them.

Because spirits were supposed to fly only in straight lines it was regarded as advisable for city gates to be built not quite opposite each other, or else with an obstruction of some sort between them. The long straight streets of Chinese cities, for example, were broken with ornamental arches off which the spirits were believed to bounce harmlessly. Similarly a 'spirit wall' was often built just inside the main gate that led into the courtyard of a home – this was meant to prevent the spirits from getting in.

As it was also well known that ghosts could not pass through a circle – emblematic of the sacred sun – round doors and windows were sometimes used. Nailing long, narrow leaves over a doorway likewise gave protection, because ghosts were believed to mistake them for swords. Stone guardian lions were thought to work especially well – but were regrettably very expensive.

Other protective devices included mirrors poised over the main gate to a home – supposedly, the spirits would be repelled by their own ugly faces. Tigers were believed to frighten off spirits, so children were dressed in cloth hats depicting tigers and wore shoes with little cloth tiger faces. They sometimes wore silver amulets around their necks shaped like locks to 'lock' them to life.

Because ghosts were also allegedly frightened by sudden loud noises, large sums were spent on firecrackers to keep them away from weddings and funerals and to ensure that travellers got off to a safe start on a long journey – you let off the crackers at the time of departure. Further protection might be sought by following a circuitous route to create confusion about one's destination.

Children were supposed to be particularly vulnerable to ghosts which led in some cases to gruesome treatment. The body of a dead infant might be crushed into an unrecognisable mess of flesh and bones to imprison whatever spirit had taken possession of it and caused its death. A dying child might be put outside the house to expire, so that its ghost would not be able to find its way back in. To protect a sole male heir from abduction into the ether he might be called by a girl's name or even adorned with earrings. Another ploy was to get him technically adopted by another family so that a vengeful demon would be unable to discover his true lineage.

---

beating the image of a city rain god with a bamboo cane to persuade it into action during a drought.

Taoist mythology was another rich source of deities, such as the fearsome Lei Gong, Duke of Thunder, worshipped by people longing for revenge. One of his jobs was to punish those – mortals and spirits alike – who had been guilty of secret crimes. He and his assistants, such as Feng Popo (Madame Wind), Yun Tong (Cloud Youth) and Tian Mu (Mother of Lightning), were also believed to control the weather. A more benign figure in the Taoist pantheon was Xi Wang Mu (Queen Mother of the West), believed to reign over a paradise-like realm in the Kunlun Mountains along Tibet's northern border.

Mythological creatures, meanwhile, included the phoenix, the unicorn and, of course, the dragon (*long*). For the Chinese the dragon was a beneficent, rather than a fearsome, creature, a symbol of imperial dignity and the empire as a whole. Among the blessings it was believed to dispense was rain.

HEAVENLY HAVOC The war god Guan Di wields a halberd and is accompanied by a banner-bearer. The god was originally a mortal, the chivalrous hero Guan Yu who lived in the 3rd century AD. He was deified in 1594.

THE WORLD OF GHOSTS
The Chinese believed firmly in ghosts, the spirits of those who had no descendants to worship them or whose worshippers did so inadequately. Some ghosts, the

spirits of the unburied such as soldiers who had died away from home, were permanent wanderers. They were always hungry and often ill-disposed towards the living. To ward them off, people adopted a number of practices. The most important was to leave food offerings at the back door on the 2nd and 16th days of each lunar month – the times when the ghosts were believed to return to their

SOMETHING TO CELEBRATE

FOR A SOCIETY that honoured the Confucian virtues of diligence and frugality, imperial China also celebrated a wide range of festivals – although there was no official weekly day of rest to correspond to the Christian Sunday.

The New Year Festival – falling in late January or early February, its exact dates calculated according to the lunar calendar – was observed by all classes and regions. It lasted for 15 days and was the major opportunity for family reunions and visits to friends. Feasting was an important part of such occasions, so that even the poorest tried to put meat, dumplings and other comparatively rich fare on the table. As New Year fell in midwinter, there was little to be done in the fields allowing even the hardest-working peasant some respite from his labours. While merchants reckoned their year-end accounts, the kitchen god in each household was bribed with sacrifices to encourage him to give a favourable account of the family to the heavenly Jade Emperor. The New Year break ended on the 15th day of the first month with displays along every street of ornamental paper lanterns, shaped like dragons, boats and animals. They were inspected by women of all classes on one of the few occasions when even the ultra-respectable were permitted to promenade freely in public.

The Qingming ('Clear and Bright') festival, usually falling around April 5, was another occasion for family solidarity, but this time across generations, as dutiful adults visited and cleaned the graves of their ancestors. The Dragon Boat Festival of the fifth day of the fifth month (early June in our calendar) was marked by boat races on rivers and canals. People also bought charms to ward off summer ailments. In autumn the festival of the 15th day of the eighth month (roughly September) focused on viewing the harvest moon and eating 'moon cakes', while the ninth day of the ninth month meant finding a hilly spot, with a fine outlook, from which to picnic. This commemorated an ancient legend about a man named Fei Changfang living under the later Han dynasty (AD 25-221). He was warned that disaster would strike him unless he climbed up a hill, which he did. When he returned home, he found his oxen, sheep, dogs and other animals lying dead . . . but he had escaped.

In each region, town and village the cycle of major festivities that were celebrated throughout China was punctuated with local festivals. Sacred sites in each region also attracted regular expeditions of pilgrims. Less happily, droughts or epidemics might prompt public offerings and special ceremonies to invite the gods to intervene.

Festival celebrations helped to support not only monks and priests but also a sizable handicraft industry turning out candles, incense, banners, statues, parasols, souvenir pictures, special foodstuffs and 'spirit money' which was transmitted to the gods by burning.

family homes. Sometimes a washbasin and cloth was left out for them as well.

Other ghosts spent most of the year confined to the limbo of the spirit world. Their great moment was the Festival of Hungry Ghosts which came in the seventh month – roughly our August. By tradition this was a month when the Gates of Hell were opened and the ghosts were free to roam about among the living. During the month more elaborate food offerings than usual were placed for them outside the temples, and Buddhist priests

IN THE AFTERLIFE A Buddhist temple is the setting for one of the rites celebrating a dead person's passage through the afterlife. These were occasions for joy rather than grief provided the family had fulfilled the correct procedures. Here the widow distributes sweets to children.

were employed to perform ritual ceremonies designed to placate them. Large coloured paper models of houses, horses and carriages were also erected to provide the ghosts with some comforts.

Taoist and Buddhist priests often officiated at festivals and at some family occasions such as funerals, but there was also a wide range of 'religious' professionals outside the priesthood. They included diviners who foretold the future from sticks tossed onto a table or the floor or from paper slips picked out by trained birds. There were also astrologers who told your horoscope.

VIRTUE IS REWARDED **This temple in Macao honours Ah Ma, a poor Fujianese girl who begged successive captains for a passage home. One eventually granted her request and obtained his reward during the voyage when the ship survived a terrific typhoon.**

RELIGION WITHOUT PRIESTS

Many religious rites were carried out without any help at all from priests or other professionals. They included the rituals of ancestor worship, the worship of household gods such as the Stove God and certain festivals, such as the Qingming festival when family graves were cleaned and tended and offerings of food presented to the ancestors and then eaten as a picnic.

Some people had an affinity with a particular religion (Buddhism, say) or a particular deity and so frequented the relevant temples or shrines. Others were spurred on by need. The Temple of the Eastern Peak in Beijing, for example, had a shrine to the Princess of the Coloured Clouds, believed to help childless mothers and sick children.

In contrast to these more domestic devotions were the vast public celebrations that were an essential part of the temple fairs. These were held at different times in all parts of China on the special days devoted to individual temple gods. Such fairs attracted thousands, or tens of thousands, of visitors. During the three, four or five days of each festival there were long, loud and colourful processions led

by robed Buddhist or Taoist monks accompanied by gongs, music and clouds of incense. There were massive food offerings spread out for the gods and spirits and for the human participants, for whom elaborate feasting was always part of the delights of the fairs.

There were fireworks and firewalking displays, as well as hundreds of market stalls with the usual accompaniment of storytellers, puppet-shows, jugglers, acrobats and magicians. The writer H.Y. Lowe left a vivid description of the stalls at a Beijing temple fair and the goods they sold: 'The most popular souvenirs are . . . little charms made of red chenille which each visitor to the temple buys and fastens to the hat or in the hair in the case of a woman. . . . Red hawthorns, strung onto wicker sticks . . . and smeared over with sugar, are the edible speciality of a few stalls . . . and paper butterflies coloured with weird effects and mounted on bare branches of willow are offered by others. While still another group of pedlars offers . . . windwheels made of coloured paper and mounted on a framework of cornstalks.' These were occasions for men, women and children alike – fair, market, carnival, festival and religious ritual all rolled into one.

CONVERT OR STARVE

During a famine in 1877 French Catholic missionaries insisted on conversion before they would give aid to famished refugees – and gained more than 100 000 new members for their congregations.

In 1890 China's 1296 Protestant missionaries, representing 130 different denominations from 13 countries, had only 37 000 communicants to minister to.

ALLAH'S ALLIES: MUSLIMS IN CHINA

COMMUNITIES of Arab and Persian Muslims were established in the trading cities of southern China from as early as the 8th century AD.

Five centuries later the conquering Mongols brought in Muslims from the sultanates of central Asia to serve them as soldiers and officials. As trusted allies many of the Muslims' fellow believers from central Asia were permitted to settle in western frontier areas, where they worked in the caravan trade, as drovers of and dealers in camels and as traders in such goods as jade, felt and leather. Gradually they came to identify themselves more closely with Chinese ways. They spoke Chinese, bore Chinese names and wore Chinese dress, although remaining Muslims.

During the decline of the Qing dynasty in the 19th century, Islamic revivalist movements found some support among these Chinese Muslims. This was partly a result of the activities of missionaries from central Asia and beyond. The so-called New Teaching called for Muslims to return to an Islam purged of contaminating Chinese influences and to assert their independence from alien overlordship. The empire's gathering economic and social ills made this a more attractive and realistic prospect.

The Chinese Muslims were divided by the New Teaching movement's denunciations of their traditional version of Islam. Some were loyal to the old ways; others responded enthusiastically to the new creed. Large-scale revolts occurred in provinces where Muslims constituted a high proportion of the population, such as Gansu, where one person in three was a Muslim, and in Shaanxi and Xinjiang. In Yunnan, a New Teaching leader Du Wenxiu, assuming the title 'Sultan Suleiman', governed a secessionist Muslim state for 15 years before it was finally crushed by imperial forces.

Alarmed by these destructive outbursts, the central government in 1884 amended the status of sprawling Xinjiang, first annexed to the Chinese Empire in the 1750s, changing it from a military colony to an integral province of the country, with a civil administration of its own. This policy, which meant tighter control from Beijing, failed to eradicate unrest in the north-west of the empire for the rest of the dynasty's existence. The Muslims of China's frontier regions never abandoned their separate identity – or their craving for autonomy.

STRONGHOLD OF FAITH This mosque stood in Gansu province, where a third of the population was Muslim. Mosques also served as schools, libraries, law courts and communal meeting-places.

ISLAND OF TRANQUILLITY

NATURE and artifice combine to soothe the soul in this city garden. A lady emerges from the verandah of a pavilion to bring tea to the gentlemen, intent on their game. Two more ladies appreciate the mock-mountain wilderness set off by the stout outer wall and inhabited by an imaginary population of monsters and demons, represented by artfully arranged boulders. The gardener and his assistant unobtrusively tend a bed of flowering shrubs. The precise angularity of the lattice windows, balustrade and paving stones contrasts pleasingly with sweeping lines of foliage and the soft tendrils of new growth.

The creator of such a garden was undoubtedly showing off his expertise and aesthetic sense as he chose and placed his plants and selected the most appropriate rocks and pots to set them off. A classic garden represented time, taste, toil and treasure – but it was a work of art worthy to rank with the poems or paintings that gardens so frequently inspired.

CRIME AND PUNISHMENT

To the minds of Chinese mandarins, shaped by the Confucian tradition, anarchy was

the worst of evils. Where good manners failed to keep bad impulses in check,

stronger measures were clearly justified.

RULES ABOUT CRIME and punishment were laid down in meticulous detail and reflected the Chinese view of society as a male-dominated pyramid, with the emperor at the apex and the family at the base. Fragments of a legal code dating from 221 BC in the times of the Qin dynasty survive, and it is clear that even then the idea of a rigid penal code detailing crimes and specifying punishments was well established.

At the start of the Qing era, the legal code of the Ming dynasty was reviewed and revised by a committee whose work received imperial approval in 1647. By the time the British diplomat John Barrow

THE EMPEROR'S EYE The calm and order of this idealised scene is guaranteed by the diligence and wisdom of the magistrate (bottom right), dispensing justice against kneeling ne'er-do-wells.

SLICED TO DEATH – BY INCHES AND MINUTES

IN JULY 1851 the British interpreter Thomas Taylor Meadows witnessed the execution of 34 rebels at Guangzhou (Canton). Thirty-three were decapitated, but for their leader an even more terrible death was decreed – *lingchi*, 'death by 1000 cuts':

❛ [The] executioner proceeded, with a single-edged dagger or knife, to cut up the man on the cross . . . As the man was at the distance of 25 yd [23 m], with his side towards us, though we observed the two cuts across the forehead, the cutting off of the left breast, and slicing of the flesh from the front of the thighs, we could not see all the horrible operation. From the first stroke of the knife till the moment the body was cut down from the cross and decapitated, about four or five minutes elapsed. We should not have been prohibited from going close up, but as may easily be imagined, even a powerful curiosity was an insufficient inducement to jump over a number of dead bodies and literally wade through pools of blood, to place ourselves in the hearing of the groans indicated by the heaving chest and quivering limbs of the poor man. Where we stood, we heard not a single cry.... ❜

LAST MINUTES Condemned criminals, restrained by their pigtails, await death by strangulation. The board between them will proclaim their crime.

visited China in the late 18th century he was impressed to see that the laws could be referred to in '15 published volumes in the plainest characters that the language will admit'. He noted that they were grouped under headings and each was accompanied by a summary and a short specimen case.

In China, unlike England, however, there was no scope for individual cases to be used to establish legal precedents. Chinese law was an inflexible system that attempted to be so detailed and precise that it encompassed every situation that could possibly arise. This level of precision applied to all crimes, from the heinous to the trivial.

At the top of this scale were crimes committed against the emperor. Thus anyone entering the Forbidden City without permission would incur 100 blows of the bamboo while any stranger found within the emperor's apartments was doomed to death by strangulation. Treason and rebellion attracted the severest penalty of all – *lingchi*, or 'death by 1000 cuts' – a slow, lingering process that not only ensured an excruciatingly painful death, but completely destroyed the condemned man's body.

The other main methods of capital punishment were beheading and strangulation. Strangulation, despite being a slower and more painful death than decapitation, was considered a milder punishment because it left the body intact. Since a person's body was regarded not as a personal possession but as a bequest from his ancestors, to mutilate it, or allow it to be mutilated, was considered unfilial behaviour.

The very young and the very old, those under the age of seven and over the age of 90, were exempt from punishment for all crimes except treason and rebellion.

NOTIONS OF LAWFULNESS

The function of the law in Chinese society was to guide everyone's activity in the direction most favourable to the state. Western observers noted that there was no concept of justice for the individual. For the Chinese the law implied a harsh and unbending system of control and ordinary people greatly distrusted it. Litigation was seen as harsh and expensive and something to be avoided wherever possible.

Chinese law recognised the family as the basic unit of society and many of its provisions were designed to bolster its survival and cohesion. This, for

115

SEEN TO BE DONE Punishment for rebels was often swift, summary and highly public as in this decapitation.

the lawmakers, meant a bias in favour of age, men and senior generations. The bias towards men was clearly seen in the laws affecting marriage. These allowed a man to rid himself fairly easily of an unwanted wife – or to take a concubine – whereas a wife who ran away from her husband would be punished with 100 strokes of the bamboo. If a wife beat her husband she would be sentenced to a flogging of 100 strokes; if she caused him permanent injury she would be strangled; if she killed him she would be beheaded. By contrast, the maximum penalty a husband could receive if he killed his wife was strangulation (not beheading).

The different degrees of kinship (*wufu*) were also enshrined in the law, which enforced the duties of mourning within these degrees – though punishments were laid down only if you failed to mourn properly for someone higher up the scale. Thus a son could be punished for failing to carry out the mourning rituals due to his father, but there

was no punishment for a father who failed to mourn for a dead son. The point was to reinforce the authority and influence of the head of the household and the men in the senior generations of the family.

Punishments, too, were graded to reflect this priority. The legal code stated that a 'son who strikes

RESTORING DOMESTIC HARMONY A husband beats his wife. Beyond high walls neighbours listen in with unabashed interest. A husband was punished for beating his wife only if injury resulted.

116

EYEWITNESS

BEARING WITH THE BARBARIANS

FOR THE CHINESE the ceremonials of formal politeness were more than just a question of manners – they were a technique for keeping social chaos at bay. Regrettably, even supposedly educated Westerners found this impossible to grasp, as Qiying, Chinese plenipotentiary for negotiating terms at the end of the Opium War of 1842, observed with fatigued disdain:

❛ Born and brought up in foreign countries, these barbarians are quite unable to understand the affairs of the Empire of the Middle [China] . . . These barbarians are very fond of their wives . . . When I went to their homes on an official call, suddenly these women appeared and greeted me. I was greatly embarrassed, but they were highly pleased. This shows plainly that it is impossible to obtain anything from these barbarians with regard to ceremonial, and that it would be useless to try to enlighten their stupidity. They also presented me with some small gifts, such as wines, perfumes etc. For my part, I made them large gifts, on the principle that he must give generously who has received little. ❜

or beats a parent suffers decapitation, irrespective of whether or not injury results. However, no penalty applies to a parent who beats his son, unless the son dies, in which case the punishment for the parent is 100 blows of the heavy bamboo if the beating was provoked by the son's disobedience, and one year of penal servitude plus 60 blows of the heavy bamboo if the beating was done wantonly.'

'No parents in the world are wrong' was a popular adage in China. Parents could have their sons punished by beating or banishment for drunkenness, laziness, gambling, disobedience, or almost any behaviour inimical to them, such behaviour being by definition unfilial.

Banishment, which completely and publicly removed the individual from the family, was regarded as the most serious punishment short of death. To the Chinese, an individual who could no longer identify with his ancestors or the living members of his family was doubly damned. It was only fathers, within the family, who had the right to call upon the state to banish their offspring and thus in this instance it was the state that acted as the agent for the parent.

Usually offences were considered more serious if they occurred between people who were related to one another than if the people were unrelated. Interestingly, however, there were some offences that were considered less serious if committed against a relative, including theft within the family. Here the closer the relationship the lighter the penalty – on the grounds that family property was regarded as being held in common anyway – and all penalties within the family were lower than for a similar theft occurring outside the family.

IMPERIAL PREROGATIVES OF MERCY

In theory and according to a tradition going back more than 1000 years, the emperor was ultimately responsible for administering justice. But this power was devolved downwards through the administrative hierarchy from province to department to district.

All cases involving sentences more severe than penal servitude had to be reported by the highest provincial authority to the Board of Punishment in Beijing and the sentences were subject to the board's approval. Similarly throughout the Qing period, all death sentences had to be referred to the board to be deliberated there by central government officials and referred to the emperor for the final decision. Only the emperor could pardon anyone who had killed another. Inevitably, in a country as vast and diverse as China, these imperial prerogatives were not always enforced and the British diplomat John Barrow commented on several instances where provincial viceroys assumed them.

Barrow, along with other Western observers, was struck by the sacredness usually attached to human life in China ('except in the horrid practice of exposing infants'). He noted, for example, that a 'murder is never overlooked . . . nor dares the

WINNOWING FOR WISDOM An examination is under way to select magistrates for service in rural parts of the empire.

emperor himself – all-powerful as he is – to take away the life of the meanest subject, without the formality at least of a regular process'.

Except during emergencies, such as rebellions when summary executions might in practice be undertaken by provincial authorities, criminals condemned to execution were always taken to appear before the highest judicial tribunal in Beijing where appeals were considered. Executions were usually carried out, at intervals, on several criminals at once. George Staunton, who was secretary to Lord Macartney's embassy to China in 1793-4, was impressed by the small numbers involved – 'seldom above 200, which is very small for so vast and populous an empire'.

LOCAL JUSTICE

For the myriad of lesser offences that did not attract the death penalty, district magistrates were given the job of judging the case and dealing out any punishment. In several respects their responsibilities were extremely wide. Xie Jinhuan, an instructor in a

118

government district school in the 1820s, remarked that there were only two groups of important officials in the empire: the grand secretaries (heads of the various government boards) in the capital and the district magistrates outside the capital.

The magistrates heard all cases that came up within their districts. They conducted the proceedings and came to their decisions virtually unaided. They also conducted investigations and inquests, and acted as detectives tracking down criminals. Beyond that, however, their task was fairly limited. They had to establish what crime had been committed and then refer to the code of laws for the scale of crimes and punishments. There was no possibility of taking the character or circumstances of the accused into account. There were no juries to give a verdict and no advocates to present the cases for and against the accused.

Advice when it was available was provided by a private secretary, employed directly by the magistrate to help him with his duties and to provide specialist advice on such topics as law and taxation. A private secretary was often recruited from among the many scholars struggling to pass through the system of public examinations. He would usually live within the magistrate's official residence, or *yamen*, and his tasks included preparing case summaries for the magistrate. Private secretaries were not, however, allowed into the courts while a case was being heard.

On such occasions the magistrate would wear his most formal robes and sit on a raised dais at one end of a hall behind a bench covered with red cloth. On this bench stood his official seal, writing brushes, inkstone (a carved stone used for grinding and mixing ink) and relevant documents. There was a cylindrical holder

JUDGE AND JURY **The English traveller Peter Mundy sketched this scene in the 1630s. In Chinese law, enquiry, verdict and sentence were all in the hands of the judge.**

ORDER IN CHINATOWN

A defeated uprising in 1853 led China's secret societies to establish 'chapters' in North America. The rising was led by an offshoot of the Triads. The rebels fled abroad to cities such as San Francisco where they won recruits among the local Chinese population. Their activities were often Mafia-like – on the other hand, San Francisco's Chinatown was more orderly than any other part of the city.

containing bamboo spills that could be thrown on the floor to indicate the number of strokes to be given if the accused was sentenced to be beaten.

The magistrate was usually attended by a clerk and a number of 'runners', all of whom, unlike the private secretaries, were government employees. The clerks were notorious for the way they manipulated the system and deceived the overworked magistrates. Thus one 19th-century authority, Feng Guifen, remarked 'if a magistrate says "yes", and the clerk says "no", the result will be "no" '. The clerks mainly came from the property-less class and were often guilty of extorting money from people within the magistrate's district in order to support themselves and their families.

The runners, meanwhile, provided communication with the various villages under the magistrate's jurisdiction. In court they also guarded the prisoners and administered torture and punishments as required. Not surprisingly they were feared and despised. Referred to as 'the claws and teeth' of the magistrates, they were looked down on socially – some lineages even expelled any member who took up such a post.

Torture was an accepted part of the judicial system. Magistrates were authorised to use it to obtain confessions from suspects, except when the person under interrogation was over 70, under 15 or an invalid. The permitted forms of torture included flogging, slapping and 'squeezing' of fingers or ankles. The equipment used included an unpleasant array of whips, ankle-screws and bamboo rods of various sizes and thicknesses. All instruments of torture had to conform to various regulations regarding their size and form and had to be officially examined and branded by the senior magistrate in the district.

While a case was being heard, it was customary not only for the accused but for everyone else involved, including the witnesses, to kneel on the ground in front of the magistrate. There was also often an audience of any members of the public who cared to attend. This was encouraged as it was thought to help to preserve social order.

INSTRUMENTS OF PUNISHMENT

The most common sentences consisted of fines and various degrees of corporal punishment. Since sentences were intended to provide salutary warnings to others as well as to injure those condemned, they were frequently inflicted in public.

Staunton described how a wooden collar known as the *cangue* was generally administered for petty crimes: 'It consists of an enormous tablet of wood with a hole in the middle to receive the neck and two smaller ones for the hands of the offender. It is a kind of permanent and ambulatory pillory, which the culprit is sentenced sometimes to wear for weeks or months together. He is suffered, provided his strength will enable him, to walk about; but he is frequently glad, for the support of this awkward and degrading burden, to lean against a wall or a tree. If a servant or a runner of the civil magistrate takes it into his head that the culprit has rested too long, he beats him with a whip made of leather thongs till he rises.'

Being beaten with bamboo rods of specified thickness was probably the most common punishment. The district magistrate was not the only person authorised to inflict such beatings. All government officers had the power to inflict summary punishment with the bamboo and, as Barrow commented, such whippings were a frequent sight: 'In travelling through the country, a day seldom escaped without our witnessing the applicating of the bamboo, and

WOODEN COLLAR The cangue was a relatively mild punishment, for crimes such as petty thefts. The wearer could not feed himself and had to rely on the kindness of passers-by. Cards on the collar proclaimed his offence.

CAGE OF DEATH An immobilised criminal is left to die of starvation, exposure and exhaustion, his crime proclaimed to passers-by as a warning. The picture was taken by the Scot John Thomson around 1870.

generally in such a manner that it might be called by any other name except a gentle correction.'

The main categories of punishment – death, corporal punishment and banishment – all brought public disgrace on the families of the criminals and derived much of their force precisely from this disgrace. The prison system in China never succeeded in linking the fate of the criminal with the reputation of his family in the same way. Jails functioned more as a repository for those awaiting trial or transfer to a higher authority than as a place of punishment.

Although Barrow found the prisons he saw 'well kept', most other Western observers deplored the conditions. In the 1860s the British diplomat Sir Henry Parkes was thrown into a Chinese prison after being captured during the Opium Wars. He described how prisoners 'who have no means of their own were reduced by prison filth and prison diet to a shocking state of emaciation and disease; but those who could afford to fee the gaolers, and purchase such things as they wanted, lived in comparative fullness and comfort'.

PENAL REFORM

Towards the end of the Qing era in the late 19th century the Chinese became more and more sensitive to Western accusations that their legal system and punishments were barbaric. In an attempt to

EYEWITNESS

THE GRIM HUMOUR OF ADVERSITY

THE WRITER Pu Songling was born in 1640 and lived most of his life in the mountains of central Shandong, thus enduring decades of rebellions, banditry and famines. In such confused times, a belief in ghosts, demons and other malevolent spirits was commonplace. The sceptical Pu mocked credulity with sardonic humour:

❦ During the reign of the first Qing emperor so many people in our county were rebels that the magistrates did not dare to arrest them

all. When things settled down they were separately classified as "rebel households". Whenever there was a dispute between them and law-abiding people the magistrates would favour the former rebels lest they rebel again. Soon every litigant would falsely claim to be an ex-rebel to help his case and his opponent would try to disprove this, so much time was taken up investigating the claim and counter-claim before the case could even begin.

Now it so happened that the compound of one of the magistrates was plagued with fox spirits who bewitched his daughter, so he sent for a shaman. The shaman bewitched the fox spirits and trapped them in a bottle, which he corked and then held over the fire. As he was about to drop it into the flames the voice of a fox spirit could be heard quite distinctly from within the bottle – "You can't do this to me! I'm from a rebel household!" ❧

OPIUM'S DEADLY DREAM

THE CHINESE USED OPIUM as a medicine and aphrodisiac for 1000 years before they took to mixing it with tobacco and smoking it in the early 17th century – when tobacco first arrived from America. Smoking the tobacco-opium mix seems to have begun among Chinese living in South-east Asia, then spread to Taiwan and the southeastern mainland. A first attempt to prohibit the drug was made in 1729 – and many times thereafter.

By the 1760s opium was being smoked pure and, during the next few decades, its use spread inland. Transport workers putting in long hours of backbreaking effort used it as a food substitute and painkiller. Soldiers, merchants and officials used it as a source of cheap pleasure. By 1800 large-scale and illegal importing of opium was big business on China's southern coast, egged on by British merchants who made vast profits from the trade.

Despite official efforts to block imports, by the 1830s the trade was so extensive that it had reversed China's formerly favourable balance of payments, and the 4000 chests a year of 1800-20 had become more than 40 000 chests a year, accounting for more than half of all British exports to China –

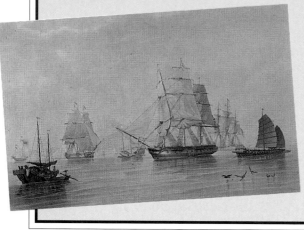

CORROSIVE CARGO
Western ships bringing opium from India in 1824. Addiction came to be the social cancer of 19th-century China.

the opium was grown in British-ruled India. Exports of tea and silk alone could not pay for the inflow, so there was a massive outflow of silver, which depressed the economy of south China.

Addiction affected all social classes, even eunuchs in the Forbidden City and members of the imperial family. When imperial troops failed to quell a rebellion in Guangdong in 1832 their failure was blamed on opium addiction. By the 1880s perhaps 15 million were addicted, the chief offenders being the educated classes, who had the time and money to indulge.

Official attempts to break up distribution networks were frustrated by corruption. Too many – suppliers, dealers, financiers and users – were committed to the trade for it to be easily smashed. The campaign for suppression continued after the fall of the Qing dynasty, long after foreign supplies had been supplanted by domestic ones.

---

demonstrate that their nation was modernising and humane, Chinese delegations began to attend European conferences on penal reform and to alter their laws along Western lines.

One reformist official argued in favour of a sharper distinction between the treatment for serious criminals and petty offenders. Those in jail for debt should, he suggested, be given 'a metal bed, blankets and pillows. All should be clean and [bed linen] changed once a week'. He was also strongly in favour of criminals doing some kind of labour service, such as repairing China's notoriously bad roads. Some changes were indeed introduced. During the final days of the Chinese Empire many

CORNERSTONE OF GOOD ORDER The father dominated the family, and the family was the fundamental building block of a stable and orderly society. To murder one's father was therefore the most heinous of all crimes.

corporal punishments were converted into fines or prison terms and in 1907 the whole prison system was overhauled and given more prominence as a punishment.

POWER AND AUTHORITY

China, in the eyes of the Chinese, lay at the centre of the world and the imperial court lay at the centre of China. A world set apart by its seclusion, ritual, pomp and luxury, the court went on its stately, scholarly way, observing codes that had been laid down for centuries, long before the Qing dynasty came to power. The mandarin scholar-bureaucrats who ran the empire similarly operated according to time-honoured values that did not necessarily include an appreciation of administrative talent.

THE SON OF HEAVEN

The emperor's life was shrouded in ritual, keeping him at an awesome distance from

his subjects. Officially at least, they were supposed to prostrate themselves even

when they encountered his portrait or photograph.

THE CALAMITIES that overtook China from the middle of the 19th century onwards destroyed a 2000-year-old empire. Yet oddly enough, daily life at the imperial court in Beijing remained relatively unchanged. In fact, as China weakened, its rulers retreated farther and farther into the apparent safety of their empire's ancient traditions. The Confucian state was never more Confucian than in its twilight period. The foreigners who did so much to bring down the empire did not find themselves confronted by a nation in arms led by a patriotic ruler. Instead the rulers applied themselves ever more determinedly to scholarship, piety and the study of ancient texts. Court ritual was reinforced and the emperor's status as ruler of 'all under heaven' underlined, even as it became more and more absurd.

Curiously, the Manchus, though they had conquered by the sword, increasingly lost the habit of ruling by it. They denigrated the virtues of the military and exalted those of scholarship. They sought to rule as sages, as Confucius had demanded. Above all, they claimed to rule not by right of conquest but by the ancient doctrine of the Mandate of Heaven, the belief that Heaven conveyed authority to a good ruler. As it happened, this was a two-edged weapon: on the one hand, it sanctified the throne; on the other, it meant that those occupying it did so only for as long as Heaven approved. The very fact that a dynasty collapsed, as dynasties frequently did in Chinese history, meant that the mandate had been withdrawn – it had passed, perfectly legitimately, to a usurper or successor.

RULER BEHIND THE SCREEN

While he ruled, however, the emperor was Heaven's representative on Earth. As such his position was unique. At audiences his ministers prostrated themselves before a screen which hid him from view.

When he left Beijing for his summer palace he travelled along a route covered with sand of the imperial colour, yellow, and constructed for him and his entourage alone. When it was unavoidable to pass bystanders, his subjects prostrated themselves.

When he ate he ate alone, and he ate off plates of imperial yellow. Indeed, that colour singled him out in countless ways from ordinary mortals. The last emperor Pu Yi was struck by it: 'The glazed tiles were yellow, my sedan chair was yellow, my chair cushions were yellow, the linings of my hats and clothes were yellow, the girdle around my waist was yellow, the dishes and bowls from which I ate and drank, the padded cover of the rice-gruel saucepan, the material in which my books were wrapped, the window curtains, the bridle of my horse . . . everything was yellow. This colour, the so-called "brilliant yellow", was used exclusively by the imperial household and made me feel from my earliest years that I was unique and had a "heavenly" nature different from that of everybody else.'

In fact, the emperor's life was a reflection, albeit on a vastly enlarged scale, of the lives expected of his subjects. Thus he worshipped his ancestors and absorbed the classics. As a good Confucian he knew that the reverence of his subjects was for his throne, not for him as a person. His job was not to direct but to set an example. His personal virtues ideally lay in piety, diligence and listening to his ministers.

PRISONER OF THE SYSTEM? **Surrounded by a complex hierarchy of officials, eunuchs, guards and slaves, an emperor could easily become imprisoned by the routines and rituals of the Forbidden City (below).**

HEAVEN'S GATES Warriors and scholars gather outside the Forbidden City. Trespassing within its boundaries was a criminal offence subject to severe penalties.

Certainly he was supposed to choose good ones but then to follow their advice.

For the emperor, to be 'active' was unnecessary in the view of the Confucian scholars. According to the ancient texts: 'He who is the ruler of men takes non-action as his way . . . He sits upon the throne of non-action and rides upon the perfection of his ministers. His feet do not move but his ministers lead him forward.' Again: 'The people are of most importance; the spirits of the land and grain are next; and the sovereign is insignificant.'

The emperor studied such texts all his life. One of the most remarkable of the Qing rulers, the Kangxi Emperor (who reigned from 1662 to 1722), kept scholars in constant attendance in his library, and he was not trying to make up for any lack of study in his youth. As a young man at the Palace School for Princes he had worked for years from 5 am till 4 pm with few breaks, focusing on classics, histories, the Mongol and Manchu languages and verse composition.

Just as youthful emperors and heirs started their schooling at an early hour, so when they came of age they conducted government business early in the day. The gates of the Forbidden City opened at midnight and the Audience Halls at 2 am. Audiences began before dawn, and all government business, including court rituals and recreation was designed to be over by 11 am.

A TIME TO REJOICE

Like the rest of the population the emperor or heir-apparent had his marriage partner chosen for him by his parents, in practice his mother. Her choice always fell on a highborn Manchu girl and it was likely to be dictated by a combination of court connections and palace intrigue.

The emperor's mother also chose his 'secondary wives', or concubines, who were in turn ordered in different 'ranks'. They, too, were highborn Manchu ladies (there could be no risk of mixed blood among the imperial offspring), one of whom would normally become empress if the first wife died. These girls were selected after a complicated process which included studying their portraits, a visit by palace emissaries and the meticulous checking of their horoscopes by court astrologers. Finally they were personally inspected for their looks, qualities and health by the emperor's mother.

One of the Xianfeng Emperor's concubines, in the fifth and lowest rank, was Ci Xi (Tz'u-hsi) who, in a way that had few precedents in Chinese history, used this relatively humble position as a launching pad for much higher things. She had the good fortune to give birth to the emperor's only son, Zaichun, who at the age of six in 1862 succeeded his

THE COLOUR YELLOW Imperial yellow dominates this scene as it would all others in the Chinese emperor's daily round. The eunuch serving the food would have tasted it first – for flavour as well as poison.

THE KANGXI EMPEROR: AN IDEAL RULER

BORN IN 1654, the second Qing ruler, the Kangxi (K'ang-hsi) Emperor, came to the throne in 1662 and reigned until his death in 1722. His reign name meant 'Peaceful Harmony', and if his reign often proved warlike as he pushed back and secured the empire's frontiers, at least he could claim harmony as his longer-term aim.

The emperor set a personal example of diligence and frugality. Rising before dawn, he began the day by listening to an exposition of a text from the Confucian classics. Audiences with officials began at 7 am in spring and summer, at 8 am in autumn and winter. Routine administrative reports were dealt with first, then pressing matters of state policy, then the household concerns of the palace, finally audiences with high-ranking officials from the provinces and foreign envoys. Afternoons and evenings were spent perusing more reports or in cultural pursuits such as poetry, calligraphy or studying Western science under the guidance of a Jesuit tutor. It was usually midnight before the emperor retired, having dealt with scores of officials and an average of 300 documents in the course of a normal day.

Unlike many other emperors, the Kangxi Emperor was strong enough to avoid becoming a prisoner of his own machinery of government and energetic enough to escape from the confines of his palace. A man of exceptional physical strength and a fine archer, he was also an excellent strategist in war and an inspiring commander, crushing a major revolt by over-mighty vassals in the south, pushing back Russian incursions along the Siberian frontier

YOUNG ... The Kangxi Emperor succeeded his father aged six.

... AND OLD His 60-year reign was one of China's longest.

and adding Tibet, Taiwan and Outer Mongolia to the empire.

He was aware of the importance of waterways to his subjects and gave a high priority to dredging and embanking the Huang He (Yellow River) to stabilise its flow and to repairing the Da Yunhe (Grand Canal) that linked the south with Tianjin (Tientsin) south-east of Beijing. This meant that rice from the fertile south could be transported efficiently to the northern capital.

Keen to impress local officials with his commitment to good government, the emperor also made lengthy provincial tours of inspection, travelling six times to the south, four to the north and four to the west. Corruption and incompetence were punished with severity.

In his love of learning this Manchu emperor proved more Chinese than the Chinese. In 1677 he set up his own personal academy of picked scholars within the Forbidden City and in 1678 instituted a new programme to recruit 50 of the most brilliant scholars in the empire

for his personal service. He not only funded massive scholarly projects in which dictionaries, encyclopaedias and multi-volume chronicles were compiled but also insisted on composing personal prefaces for each as it came to publication.

The Kangxi Emperor was also alive to the practical value of European skills. He opened Guangzhou (Canton) and three other ports to foreign trade, stimulating an industrial boom in the lower Chang Jiang (Yangtze) region. He also shrewdly employed Jesuit fathers to organise the official calendar of the empire, cast cannon for his army, serve him as diplomatic interpreters and compile a massive atlas of his domains.

The Kangxi Emperor was aware that 'one act of negligence may cause sorrow all through the country and one moment of inattention may result in trouble for hundreds and thousands of generations'. He therefore drove himself and his servants hard. Having achieved a reign outlasting the auspicious number of 60 years, he died rich in honour.

IMPERIAL APPROACH Two mandarins are carried in palanquins at the northern entrance to the Imperial Palace.

father, reigning as the Tongzhi Emperor. Using her position as Empress Dowager, Ci Xi gathered huge power in her hands during her son's minority and went on to preside as China's effective ruler over the most of the final period of the Manchu Empire.

When the emperor married his principal wife there was, naturally, no question of obtaining her family's consent. An imperial edict was enough. The customary gifts made to the family on betrothal were ten horses, ten cuirasses, 100 pieces of silk and 200 pieces of Nanjing (Nanking) cloth. These gifts were brought by officials who arrived in a sedan chair ornamented with imperial dragons. When they arrived the father of the chosen bride undertook the first of many prostrations he would make in the days and months to come. On the wedding day messengers brought gifts of 200 oz (5.7 kg) of gold, 10 000 oz (284 kg) of silver, and 20 horses for the bride, with further gifts for the parents.

The bride's parents did not have a monopoly of prostrations – the emperor himself bowed nine times at the feet of his mother on his wedding day. The *Xiaojing*, 'Book of Filial Piety', noted: 'In order to prevent the people from treating their parents with cruelty, the emperor first sets an example by showing a dear love for his mother.' After these reverences, the emperor was carried in magnificent procession to the Hall of Great Harmony, while an envoy was sent to collect the bride.

At her home the envoy produced imperial letters and decrees, before which there were more prostrations. Then, with the bride carried in a sedan chair, her procession made its triumphal way to the Imperial City. At the gateway to the inner Forbidden City, they were greeted by porters bearing umbrellas with phoenix ornaments – emblem of the empress, as the dragon was of the emperor – who led the procession to the Hall of Great Harmony. Here the bride made her formal acts of subservience to her husband.

LIVING APART

The festivities were elaborate but once the marriage day was over, the emperor and empress saw little of each other, bound as they were by the rituals that separated the lives of men and women. The emperor's

continued on page 133

THE GREATEST REBELLION

The Taiping rebellion caused more deaths than all China's

other wars of the 19th century added together.

THE GREATEST domestic challenge ever faced by the Manchu emperors arose in southern China. Here resentment against their rule had never really died out since they seized power in the 1640s. By the mid 19th century, the situation was even more inflammable as the empire's most prosperous southern provinces were disrupted by economic recession and inflation.

The rebellion's leader was a state-examination candidate who had failed four times. Influenced by the teachings of Protestant missionaries, Hong Xiuquan became convinced that he was the younger brother of Jesus Christ. He was a member of the despised Hakka-speaking minority – descendants of northern Chinese who had emigrated to the south in the 12th and 13th centuries – and began to win converts among his fellow Hakka in Guangxi province. His appeal was particularly strong among the unemployed boatmen on the many waterways of the province, exploited peasants and miners, and deserters from the army. Under his inspiration, a league of militarised 'congregations', probably based on existing secret societies, came together as the God Worshipping Society. Hong's fellow leaders were an old schoolmate, Feng Yunshan, and another Hakka, Yang Xiuqing, an illiterate charcoal-burner by origin who was an organiser of genius.

Hong started by combating the 'demons' of Chinese popular religion, but after a while switched his mission to that of overthrowing the Manchu regime. In its place he planned to institute the *Taiping tianguo* – Heavenly Kingdom of Great Peace – with himself as emperor. His followers, the Taipings, abandoned the pigtail, an emblem of their subservience to the Manchus.

An exodus from Guangxi northwards towards the Chang Jiang (Yangtze) valley was accompanied by a division of authority among Hong (the 'Heavenly King'), Feng (the 'Southern King'), Yang (the 'Eastern King') and other 'kings' and 'assistant kings'. Although the rebels had some artillery, they had no cavalry, no medical corps and no maps. Most of their fighting was done hand-to-hand with swords, spears and staves and their victories were the product of fanatical courage and discipline, rather than military skill.

In March 1853 the Taipings captured Nanjing (Nanking), renaming it 'Heavenly Capital'. From there they attempted to impose their rule over China's richest region. Hong's reign of virtue prohibited opium, tobacco, wine, theatres, gambling and prostitution, destroyed temples and monasteries and even tried to institute a system of communal landownership. Foot-binding was

REBEL RETREAT Loyal Qing troops in orderly ranks are shown putting Taiping rebels to flight. The Qing forces are armed with firearms and bows, the rebels with more primitive swords and spears.

banned, and women were appointed to posts in the army and government. The traditional examination system was retained, but based on Christian not Confucian lines. There were also plans to introduce Western innovations such as banks, railways, newspapers, post offices, voting by ballot and a secret police.

Unfortunately for the Taipings, their leadership began to fall out. Yang, having claimed to receive personal visitations from God, tried to elevate himself to the same level as the 'Heavenly King'. Hong allied himself with 'Northern King' Wei Changhui, who killed Yang and was then killed himself by Assistant King Shi Dakai on behalf of Hong.

The Taipings were eventually brought down by the Manchu regular army, supported by regionally raised militias and the freelance 'Ever Victorious Army' officered by Westerners. Nanjing fell in 1864 – Hong poisoned himself during the siege. Most of his remaining followers were massacred. The Taiping rebellion cost an untold number of lives – perhaps 20 million. It also significantly weakened, though it failed to end, Manchu rule. Moreover, its chaotic sponsorship of Western-style reforms discredited the more systematic efforts of loyal and far-sighted mandarins as they tried to promote the military and economic modernisation of their tottering regime.

A GUNPOWDER EMPIRE

PRIMITIVE fireworks were made in China as early as the Tang period (AD 618-906), and the formula for gunpowder was first recorded in 1044. Explosives were used to decisive effect by the Song dynasty to repel Tatar raids in 1161-2. In the 1230s Mongol invaders were on the receiving end of rockets, colourfully referred to by Chinese chroniclers as 'arrows of flying fire' or 'long enemy-crushing snake'. Fragmentation bombs, grenades, piston-powered flamethrowers and poison gas were all developed as by-products of explosives technology.

Field artillery was used by the Ming emperors to smash Mongol cavalry on the northern steppes in the 15th century. Fixed cannon on both the Great Wall and ordinary city walls remained a major deterrent against northern invasions for the rest of the Ming era. Superior European cannon were also bought in from Macao via the Jesuits. A military manual of 1621 shows, too, a battery of wheelbarrow-mounted launchers for arrow-tipped rockets.

Under the Qing the use of personal firearms among the military increased and was a crucial factor in extending the empire's borders into Mongolia, Turkestan, Tibet and Taiwan. At the same time, however, the spread of handguns among the civilian population helped to undermine public order. An attempted ban on the private ownership of firearms was lifted in 1760 lest bandits be given too great an edge over the law-abiding.

Handguns were much easier to master than the technically demanding bow and other traditional weapons, so the gap between professional soldier and untrained civilian was significantly narrowed. The consequences of this became all too apparent in the rebellions that plagued the 19th century.

OLD AND NEW A foot soldier (right) carries a powerful compound bow. Even in the age of firearms it retained its value thanks to its rapid rate of fire. A Western-style arsenal (below) was established at Nanjing (Nanking) around 1868.

RURAL IDYLL **Summer retreats outside Beijing, like this one painted on silk, enabled Chinese emperors to commune with nature like any classical poet or sage. They were often prouder of their scholarship than their military feats.**

most constant companions were the eunuchs, a group who wielded enormous power and had their own hierarchy of 48 grades. The Chief Eunuch controlled the activities of the thousands who staffed the kitchens and gardens, made clothes and furniture, and worked as masons, builders, painters, decorators, librarians and polishers.

The eunuchs were powerful, rich and entirely dependent on the emperor. They were despised by the wider population for their disabilities, smell, premature ageing, falsetto voices and corruption. Their salaries were not high but every gift to the emperor and empress passed through their hands and some 20 per cent of its value remained with the eunuchs.

133

REFLECTED GLORY The Empress Dowager Ci Xi rearranges a hair ornament. During the reigns of two emperors, her son Tongzhi and her nephew Guangxu, she was China's effective ruler, in clear contravention of imperial traditions.

The household dominated by the eunuchs was indulgent, luxurious, extravagant, effeminate and rigidly structured. It was also massively overstaffed. The imperial kitchens alone employed more than 2000 people with separate departments specialising, for example, in the preparation or serving of meat, fish, turtles, wines, pickle and sauce, salt and so on.

It was, of course, the sheer extravagance of the court that most clearly isolated the emperor from his mainly impoverished people. Yet echoes of ordinary life were never far away. Emperor and court celebrated, for example, the same great festivals as the ordinary people. One such moment was the Festival of the Harvest Moon, celebrated all over China in mid autumn. In the Imperial City it was a spectacular event, with a procession of hundreds of eunuchs carrying lanterns, court grandees, prostrations to the moon and a ceremony on the lake for which the eunuchs held their lanterns in the form of the characters 'Peace' and 'Prosperity'.

NORTHERN CAPITAL

Beijing was located in the far north of China, stifling in summer but Siberian in winter when wind, snow and ice froze much of it for three or four months. The rich depended on furs which lined their boots, saddles and chairs. When the Qianlong Emperor organised a waterborne triumphal entry into the Imperial City to celebrate his mother's birthday in 1752, thousands of servants had to beat the waters of the canals to try to stop them from freezing around the processional barges. They failed and the journey was completed on sledges.

The Imperial City was a city within the city, its walls encompassing gardens and lakes to the west. Inside the Imperial City, in its turn, were the high vermilion walls, gateways and 2 mile (3.2 km) moat of the Forbidden City – so named because it was forbidden to all but the imperial family, their retainers and the highest government officials. This was a maze of palaces, temples, courtyards and gardens. As the heart of government it contained offices, storehouses, treasury vaults and armouries. Among its myriad buildings were the residences of the empress, empress or empresses dowager, eunuchs and concubines, each with their households of servants and attendants.

Yet for all its wonders, the Forbidden City was only one of many imperial residences. To the west of the Imperial City were three Sea Palaces, lapped by waters of vast artificial lakes which bordered their marbled Ocean Terraces. There was also the Summer Palace to the north of Beijing, the fabulous Yuan Ming Yuan, begun by the Kangxi Emperor, the second Qing ruler, in 1709. It was set in the fairyland Round Bright Garden with a complex of lakes, waterways, halls painted scarlet and gold, follies, artificial hills and parks. It was a paradise of animal life, with ornamental ducks, rare birds, fantailed goldfish and wandering deer.

For the hottest three months of the year, the Yuan Ming Yuan was one of the favourite residences of the Qing emperors, until it was vandalised by British and French troops in 1860 as part of sporadic hostilities between the European powers and the Manchu government during the reign of the Xianfeng Emperor. Near its site Xianfeng's former concubine, the Empress Dowager Ci Xi, later built a new Summer Palace, which became her own favourite residence – though she left the ruins of the Yuan Ming Yuan standing to act as a ghostly reminder of past splendours.

EYEWITNESS

THE LAST EMPEROR'S POST-ABDICATION STUDIES

THE LAST EMPEROR, Pu Yi, was still studying to be a good ruler at the age of 14, eight years after his enforced abdication in 1912. The republican authorities permitted him to stay in the imperial palace, where he had the finest tutors and learned English from the diplomat Reginald Johnston. One diary entry reads:

❛ Fine. Rose at four wrote out 18 sheets of the character Prosperity in a large hand. Classes at eight. Read Analects, Chou Ritual, Record of Ritual, and Tang poetry . . . Listened to tutor Chen lecturing on the General Chronological History with Comments by Qianlong Emperor. Finished eating at 9.30; read Tso Commentary, Ku-liang Commentary; heard tutor Chu on the Explanation of the Great Learning; wrote couplets. Lessons finished at 11, went to pay respects to four High Consorts [widows of previous emperors]. Johnston did not come today as he had mild flu, so returned to Heart Nurture Palace and wrote out 30 more sheets of characters Prosperity and Longevity. Read papers, ate at 4, bed at 6. Read Anthology of Ancient Literature in bed: very interesting. ❜

ILL OMEN Pu Yi stands before a screen decorated with cranes, traditionally an auspicious symbol. His reign, as the Xuantong Emperor, lasted just two years.

WORLD WITHIN WALLS

BEIJING'S Forbidden City, with its walls and moats lying at the heart of the Imperial City, betrays its origins as the armed camp of Mongol conquerors in the 13th century. Its buildings, roofed with imperial yellow tiles, conjure the ethos of a more urbane era, however, with Halls named for Supreme Harmony, Central Harmony, Protecting Harmony, Imperial Peace, Cultivation of the Mind and Vigorous Fertility and Palaces of Earthly Tranquillity and Peaceful Old Age.

The Chinese City, to the south (top right here), was the creation of the Ming Jiajing Emperor (1522-66) and was surrounded by 13$\frac{1}{2}$ miles (22 km) of walls. The Tatar City was slightly larger and lay to the north of the Imperial City. Its huge central roadway ran 5 miles (8 km) from an outer gate to the edge of the Imperial City. All walls, gates, official buildings, temples and markets were located in relation to the monumental north-south axis which ran right through the city, whose symmetry symbolised the harmonious order decreed by the ruling dynasty. Respect for tradition ensured that whenever buildings or areas were redeveloped the new version resembled the original as closely as possible.

THE POWER OF THE MANDARIN

China's scholarly elite proved to be one of the world's most enduring ruling classes.

Having passed through a gruelling series of state examinations, mandarins were

given powers of life and death over the emperor's subjects.

A CROWDED STREET in one of China's teeming cities could be frozen, at any time, by the sound of gongs and cries coming from the distance. As the noise grew louder, people struggled to clear the way, flattening themselves against the sides of the street as the mandarin procession passed by. It was led by gong beaters, followed by 'shouters' in long dresses and conical hats yelling forth the importance of their lord. Then came attendants brandishing chains like whips and finally His Excellency himself, resplendent in black robes and cap, his expression haughty as befitted a 'superior man'. He was in a sedan chair carried by the eight bearers who were officially allowed to him because of his position as a figure of the first rank.

DWELLING IN DIGNITY A mandarin's home should afford him a calm atmosphere and express his cultivation through its discreet good taste.

The greatest mandarins were awesome creatures. They were the scholar-officials who ruled the empire, owing their exalted status less to such qualities as administrative talent than to the ability to memorise vast tracts of scholarly texts. It was a scholarship no one could doubt, because they had passed through the ordeals of the state examination system.

In Europe and North America, there were celebrated doctors, lawyers, soldiers, sailors, merchants, men of business and banking, many of them rewarded with their countries' highest honours. In China, things were quite different. Here, military virtues were despised; the professions carried little status; merchants belonged to the lowest of the classes recognised by the best Confucian authorities. In official esteem scholarship reigned supreme, far above that given to the small hereditary Chinese and Manchu nobility. Scholars who had passed their examinations continued to enjoy their prestige even outside government employment.

THE ROAD TO HONOUR

These exams – theoretically open to almost every male, rich or poor – were the gateway to both official employment and family honour. Their elaborate nationwide ritual dated back to the 8th century AD at least, and demanded mastery of the Confucian classics and histories, and skills in verse composition. Successful candidates would know whole volumes of the various texts by heart. They competed against thousands of other candidates and took their exams in conditions of extreme discomfort.

The exams were held in three-year cycles. The first degree was taken in a local city. Those who

STATELY PROGRESS The noisy but splendid passage of a mandarin in his litter left onlookers in no doubt that he personified the majesty of the state and the authority of the imperial throne.

A CANDIDATE FOR FLOWERING TALENT

IT WAS still dark when Liu left his lodging house in the suburbs of the county capital. Soon he was standing with hundreds of other candidates outside the Examination Hall, within whose walls their future would be determined. They all wore red-tasselled caps without buttons.

At the entrance an imposing figure was seated, dressed in a deep blue gown and a black over-jacket.

SUPERVISED Exam procedures were meant to be strictly even-handed, but only the prosperous could afford the investment of time that successful study required.

As Prefect, supervising official of a dozen or more counties, he was responsible for more than a million of the emperor's subjects. His presence showed the government's concern that proceedings should be conducted with scrupulous fairness.

The Prefect began to call the roll. He murmured each name in a low tone, as befitted his dignity, and a junior official bawled it out. Liu presented himself in turn and passed through the compound's outer gate. Two officials frisked him, patting the thick lining of his jacket to check for the telltale rustle of concealed papers. Liu waited until he was ushered to a small cell, open-ended on the corridor side. Waiting for him was a sheaf of paper with his name written at the top on a detachable slip, and his examination number written inside. When, later, he handed his papers in he would tear off the name slip. Only after the papers had been marked would the number be revealed and, if he had been successful, posted on the hall's outer wall – the numbers would be written in a circle so that none came top or bottom.

The test consisted of recognising three quotations, placing them in their context and explaining their implications. Each quotation was written on a cube-shaped lantern which bearers carried up and down the aisles between the cells. Liu recognised the first one instantly: 'They who know the truth.' Smiling, he noted that it came from Chapter 18 of Book VI of the *Analects*.

At noon a stout official waddled down the aisle, pausing at each cell to set his seal at the point which the candidate's writing had reached. The test resumed immediately, lasting until 4 pm, when a cannon was fired. The most confident candidates, Liu among them, handed in their essays and passed out of the hall to be greeted by the town band. Then the gates were closed. At 5 pm a second call was made. At 6 there was a last call – but for the stragglers there was neither cannon nor band.

Each candidature represented years of study and the ambitious hopes of a family. Liu, who had waited for his friend Feng, could hardly bear to watch his friend's dejected figure. He decided to try the restorative powers of a meal and an evening at a travelling theatre. Looking after Feng would also stop him from worrying about the results, due in ten days' time.

passed held the degree of Flowering Talent, which entitled them to wear distinctive robes and to tax exemption. Success at this stage of the process would be celebrated at the degree-holder's home by erecting a triumphal arch or a plaque.

It did not mean employment, but it did qualify the 'flowering talents' to sit for second degrees. Exams for these were held at provincial capitals in compounds honeycombed with tiny cells in which the candidates sat. The candidates travelling to the capitals carried banners proclaiming 'Candidate for the imperially decreed provincial examinations'. These allowed them to pass freely through customs posts along the way. They brought with them food, bedding, brushes and ink for calligraphy, and were then closed off from the world for three days while they struggled with their essays.

To fail was devastating. The writer Pu Songling (1640-1716) wrote of the 'seven transformations of the candidate'. First, he was like a beggar staggering in with his luggage, then like a prisoner when searched, then the writhing larva of a bee in

DEATH FOR CHEATING

When the list of successful candidates in the local government examinations was posted up in the city of Yangzhou near the delta of the Chang Jiang (Yangtze) river in 1711, it included large numbers of sons from wealthy merchant families. This caused such indignation among more than 1000 failed students that they paraded through the city, then broke into the prefectural training college and seized its director. A nine-month investigation found the chief examiner and his colleagues guilty of accepting bribes and numerous successful candidates guilty of offering them. All were condemned to death.

he had recovered from the shock of failure, only to rail in hysterics against his examiners and Fate.

Only a handful passed – about one in a hundred. They were Recommended Men and could expect, at some future date, to be given a position such as that of district magistrate. They were also entitled to sit for the third degree in Beijing. About a quarter of the candidates for this would pass out successfully as Presented Scholars, who were finally examined in the presence of the emperor himself.

Whether the emperor personally conducted the questioning or not, all questions were asked as if he did: 'I am the Son of Heaven, responsible for governing the Empire. Night and day I wrack my brains so that the people will be able to live in tranquillity. Fortunately I have this opportunity to pose

continued on page 144

MARRIAGE OF CONVENIENCE? A mandarin from Guangzhou (Canton) sits with his wife. Badges of his rank include the silk square depicting an animal on his chest and the spike on his hat.

his cell, a tottering sick bird after the exams and a nervous monkey on a leash while waiting for his results. After that came the stage when, having learnt of his failure, he was like a motionless poisoned fly. Finally, he was like a pigeon smashing its eggs:

WISE MAN OF THE WEST

Missionary, monk and mandarin – the astute Jesuit Matteo Ricci
adapted himself to Chinese ways to win a unique position of trust.

THE ITALIAN JESUIT Matteo Ricci came to China in 1583 and remained there until his death in 1610. He was determined to earn the respect of the Chinese and did – but it took tact and time. Even his appearance was against him since he had blue eyes and a curly beard, both unknown among the Chinese. Ricci set himself diligently to learn not only the Chinese language but everything he could about Chinese customs and culture. He devised his own system for writing Chinese phonetically in Roman script, compiled his own dictionary and mastered both the spoken and classical forms of the language.

Ricci realised that any attempt at promoting Christianity and an appreciation of Western civilisation would have to be couched in terms the Chinese could sympathise with. As an expert astronomer and a mathematician, he tried to engage mandarin interest in science rather than religion, inviting cultured men to inspect his collection of clocks, globes and astronomical instruments. His deferential manner was so nicely calculated to achieve the right effect that one mandarin noted approvingly: 'He is very polite and his arguments, if challenged, are without end. Therefore, even in foreign countries, there are gentlemen.' Another mandarin helpfully suggested that Ricci exchange the robes of a Buddhist monk, which he had worn since entering China, for the dress of a scholar. When Ricci showed his new friends a

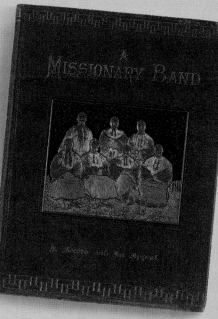

FITTING IN Decorously robed Ricci (left, on the left) stands with his convert Li Paulus. Centuries later, Protestant missionaries (above) also adopted Chinese dress to try to identify themselves with local people.

INTRUSION The spires of the French cathedral at Guangzhou (Canton) emphasise the alien origins of Christianity.

Western map of the world, they were offended that it did not show China at its centre. Ricci obligingly re-drew it and after that 'they had a much higher opinion of the European system of education'.

Ricci's diplomatic skills had earned him the right to enter inland China, usually forbidden territory for a foreigner. In 1600 he was allowed into Beijing itself. He was invited to present himself at court where, as a ritual formality, he had to bow nine times to the emperor's empty throne. Although that was as near as he ever got to the throne's occupant, Ricci was allowed to settle in the capital and was even given an allowance for living expenses.

Ricci realised that Christianity had no prospect of success if it attacked the fundamental tenets of Confucian morality. He also realised – correctly – that rituals expressing respect for ancestors were not to be equated with worshipping them as gods.

This acceptance of Chinese tradition laid the foundations for the Catholic church in China and enabled Ricci to make a number of converts among the educated classes. One, a high-ranking official known as Li Paulus, cooperated with him in translating Latin astronomical works into Chinese. When Ricci died the emperor donated land for his grave and the mayor of Beijing paid for his tombstone, which bore a fitting epitaph: 'To one who attained fame for righteousness and wrote famous books.'

HEAVENLY HARMONY Beijing's Jesuit-built astronomical observatory is depicted in a French publication of 1747.

questions to you graduates and I wish to hear your well-considered opinions on the following.' No one failed this test, but the candidates were graded and the highest passed on to the Hanlin Academy in Beijing for further study and future prospects as provincial governors, viceroys or ministers of state.

This long drawn-out process was one reason for the advanced age of the mandarin officials. At the same time, there were always more successful candidates than jobs available, a situation made worse a discriminatory employment policy. The privileged Manchus were given easier tests than the Chinese and a significant percentage of government posts were reserved for them. Nonetheless, the exams remained the normal route to government employment until their abolition in 1905.

AN ARMY OF MANDARINS

The empire employed some 40000 mandarins of varying grades – though that number was still absurdly small by modern standards. It meant that the government could never aspire to have more than one person in 10000 working directly on its behalf.

At the centre of power, advising the emperor and proposing policies every morning at daybreak, was the Grand Council, usually consisting of two Manchus, two Chinese and a Manchu chairman. There was also a cabinet of ministers, similarly granted early morning audiences. This body was entrusted with the 25 imperial seals that were used to validate the orders through which the emperor's will was transmitted to subordinate officials.

Perhaps the strangest body was the Censorate: a group of high-minded functionaries whose job was to criticise the errors of others, even of the emperor. They were also responsible – and had been for centuries – for keeping official histories of each dynasty. These were kept secret from everyone, including the emperor, until published when a dynasty fell. A record for posterity of his virtues and foibles was intended to act as a check on an emperor's conduct.

Indeed, even below the imperial level, criticism of officials was a normal feature of public life. It was a relatively common sight to see a mandarin prostrated for some offence before another mandarin of higher rank and receiving in full public view a standard number of blows with a bamboo rod.

Still at the centre of power came six boards of government. The highest of these was the Board of Civil Office which controlled recruitment into the bureaucracy. Then came the Board of Revenue with the unpopular task of raising taxes. Other boards regulated the ceremonial, sacrificial ritual and religious observances that governed much of everyday life; ran courier services, vital for keeping contact with and control of the vast empire; controlled prisons and the penal code; and were in charge of national roads, bridges and engineering projects.

There was, significantly, no Foreign Office until foreigners forced the Chinese to establish one in 1861 during a period of tension between the European powers and the Qing government. Before that foreign affairs were matters for the humble 'colonial' office which dealt with countries like Tibet, Mongolia, Korea, Annan (Vietnam) and even Japan, all of which were 'tribute kingdoms' making annual contributions to the Dragon Throne – in Japan's case until 1878.

SOVEREIGN MANDARINS

Outside the centre, China was controlled by the viceroys and governors of its 18 provinces. These men were virtual sovereigns, raising their own armies and navies and enforcing the law. Below

ROBE OF RANK This coat bears the phoenix motif of a courtier of the fifth rank. Distinctive dress called forth appropriate degrees of deference from others.

OFF DUTY   High-ranking mandarins of the Beijing Foreign Office pose for the camera in the early 1870s.

them the provinces were divided into prefectures, sub-prefectures and some 1600 districts.

It was only a district magistrate who had direct contact with the Chinese people, and he was the only mandarin without a system of departments to help him. Moreover, he was extremely badly paid – some in the north of China were paid no more than £2 a year. It was therefore not only inevitable but also accepted as normal that mandarins, high and low, would use their offices as sources of revenue. This they did through the practices of taking bribes and overcharging for tax and keeping the excess. In

fact, most mandarins lived well, but not from their salaries. In an attempt to combat growing corruption district magistrates were forbidden to hold office in their native provinces or within about 170 miles (270 km) of their home towns. The trouble with this was that the magistrate then lacked local knowledge – sometimes to the extent of not even being able to understand the local dialect.

Whatever their difficulties, the scholar-officials were still the country's elite. In China's social structure they were the gentry. Within that group, the
continued on page 149

145

THE DANCE OF THE BRUSH

Calligraphy was the supreme skill – the pathway to knowledge
and employment and the guarantor of national unity.

THE TERMS meaning 'culture' and 'writing' are the same in Chinese – a clue to the status of writing in Chinese civilisation. In imperial China, elegant calligraphy was the supreme accomplishment of a cultured man and the surest indication of the due refinement of his character.

China's earliest writing system used simple pictures to represent objects such as a mountain, tree or river. The system was then extended to encompass abstract words by compounding pictures or making loans between words that sound similar. The result was a huge multiplication of characters, each of which represented a different word. In this system, unlike an alphabetic one, a word's written form gives little or no indication of how it should be pronounced.

The system was reformed and rationalised in the interests of uniformity by the first Qin emperor in the 3rd century BC, and then remained largely unchanged until the Communist regime undertook a programme of simplification in the 1950s. For two millennia, therefore, literacy depended on the ability to master and memorise some thousands of characters, which had long since lost much pictorial resemblance to the words they stood for. It was a massive learning task for which the leisured classes had an obvious advantage, with time on their hands and access to tutors.

CALM FOR COMPOSITION A garden pavilion was considered the ideal setting for a scholar's study.

SCHOLAR SEATED Li Lianying, chief eunuch to the Empress Dowager Ci Xi, poses with the accoutrements of scholarship: brushes, an inkstone and volumes of Confucian classics and Buddhist scriptures.

YONG This character, meaning 'eternal', is made using eight brush strokes. It is frequently used to teach the arts of calligraphy. One master is said to have spent 15 years perfecting his version of it.

VENERABLE FRIENDS This portrait of six scholarly friends was painted in 1652. Like all men of education they were expert calligraphers.

Columns of characters are written in Chinese script from top to bottom and right to left. The strokes within each character are also written in a set order, from left to right. Because the ink is instantly absorbed by the mulberry paper used for calligraphy, brushwork must be both swift and faultless – 'retouching' is definitely not allowed. Brushes are always made so that the tuft comes to a sharp point, capable of making both fine and broad strokes. The skill of the individual calligrapher in creating a pleasing effect rests on such subtleties as the width of each stroke, the density of ink released from the brush (which depends on the pressure applied to it), the spacing between one character and the next and the choice of a script style appropriate to the subject matter.

The most ancient styles, known as 'Seal script' (because it was used in personal seals), have curved lines with little variation in thickness. They were originally used for writing on oracle bones used in divination or for inscriptions on bronzeware. 'Regular scripts' were derived from the bold, clear brushwork favoured by clerks in official documents. 'Running script' and 'grass script' are looser styles, in which each stroke and character flow into the next, well suited for poetry or intimate letters between friends.

INKWELL By raising and lowering a finger over the top filler, ink in the body of the pottery animal can be flowed, drop by drop, into the reservoir held in its mouth.

VANTAGE POINTS **The courtyard in a mandarin's house (left) is a miniature landscape in itself. A librarian (above) airs his stock to prevent damage from damp and insects.**

WAKING THE OLD DRAGON FROM HER SLEEP OF AGES

THE DECAY of the Chinese Empire in the late 19th century was all too evident to most Western eyes. The pioneer Scottish photographer John Thomson, however, took a more positive view of China's future:

❛ It is commonly . . . supposed in England that little or no progress is being made in China. All eyes are turned towards Japan. There it has become the fashion to discover the pet example of Eastern advancement. . . . [But] China . . . is, too, undergoing a gradual process of transition and development. Yet she esteems the philosophy of her sages as highly as in former days, and maintains her belief in the old institutions which have supported her in proud isolation and independence for so many centuries. For all that, . . . she is drifting slowly towards our Western ways . . . [Her] merchants can now boast of their Steam Navigation Companies, and . . . they are so thoroughly masters of what they have undertaken . . . as to be competing successfully with foreign companies in the carrying trade on the coast and rivers of their country. In process of time the same remark will apply to every branch of their trade and industry. China will then be able to supply not only the staple material grown on her own soil, but skilled labour and machinery to produce the fabrics which she is now obliged to import . . . Her plains are teeming with millions of poor, patient labourers, ready to turn their hands to any industry that will furnish them with the simple necessaries of life . . . Her mountains abound in metals and minerals, and her vast coal-fields are stored up to kindle the fires of a coming age of steam and iron. Western nations have woke the old dragon from her sleep of ages, and now she stands at bay, armed with iron claws and fangs of foreign steel. ❜

'upper gentry' were those who had passed the Recommended Man or Presented Scholar exams. The exam system meant that the poor could rise through academic ability, and many did. In practice, however, gentry families grew rich from their offices and used that wealth to educate their sons. Thus the majority perpetuated themselves.

The scholars of the upper gentry were a remarkable group. These were the men with long slender fingernails that made it clear they had never stooped to the indignity of manual labour. Learned and ever-courteous, they had the time and money to cultivate the arts of leisure. So, as the empire crumbled around them, they continued to study, read, write poetry, paint and perfect the delicate art of calligraphy. They owed reverence to their emperor and ancestors, but in all other ways held themselves to be, and perhaps were, Superior Men.

THE POINT OF IT ALL   A well-ordered land and people were the supposed objects of the mandarins' labours.

TIME CHART

POWER AND WEALTH

BONE OF TRUTH This oracle bone, used to obtain guidance, dates from about 1500 BC and bears an early example of Chinese writing.

c.1700-c.1028 BC The Shang dynasty presides over the earliest civilisation for which modern scholars have found archaeological evidence.

c.1027-771 BC The Zhou dynasty, originally semi-nomads, rule in western China.

481-221 BC The Warring States period, during which different states fight it out for mastery of China. The period sees the development of iron weapons, cavalry and crossbows.

221-206 BC Qin Shi Huangdi, founder of the Qin dynasty, links earlier fortifications to form the Great Wall.

206 BC Han Gao Zu founds the Han dynasty.

141-87 BC The Han emperor Wu adopts Confucian teachings, making them the state ideology.

AD 220-581 After the fall of the Han, China is split among three kingdoms.

AD 581-618 The Sui dynasty reunites north and south China and builds the Grand Canal (Da Yunhe) to link them.

AD 618-906 The Tang dynasty presides over a brilliant flowering of Chinese culture.

EMPIRE OF THE MIND A 17th-century artist showed a Han emperor supervising scholarly work on classical texts.

LEARNING, LIFESTYLE AND LEISURE

SAGE Confucius' influence spread far beyond China. This is a Japanese woodcut.

1500 BC The Chinese are using advanced techniques for casting bronze around this date.

479 BC Confucius (Kong Fuzi) dies in his native state of Lu, in the south of modern Shandong province.

289 BC Mencius (Mengzi), a follower of Confucius, dies. His teachings will earn him the posthumous title of Ya Sheng, 'Second Sage' – after Confucius.

145-90 BC The astronomer and historian Sima Qian (Ssu-ma Ch'ien) dies. His *Shi Ji* (Historical Records) is the first classic account of Chinese dynastic history.

AD 65 A Buddhist community is living at Xuzhou in the central coastal province Jiangsu – the first record of Buddhism in China.

AD 105 Around this date, a court official Cai Lun describes his method of making paper, using mulberry fibres plus rags and hemp waste.

AD 264-73 First recorded mention of tea-drinking, a habit the Chinese are fast acquiring.

AD 300 The foot stirrup, a Chinese invention, is coming into common use.

AD 868 The world's oldest surviving printed book is a Chinese Buddhist text, the Diamond Sutra.

SAINTLY FIGURE An 8th-century AD Chinese banner shows the Buddha preaching to his followers.

REST OF THE WORLD

1600 BC The Phoenicians in the eastern Mediterranean invent alphabetic writing around this time.

660 BC The date traditionally given for the accession of Jimmu, legendary first emperor of Japan.

c.483 BC Gautama Siddhartha, founder of Buddhism, dies in India.

SAVIOUR In China the spread of Christianity was inhibited by its alien origins and claims to be the sole religious truth.

438 BC The Parthenon is constructed in Athens.

323 BC Alexander the Great dies of a fever in Babylon.

AD 30 Jesus of Nazareth is crucified outside Jerusalem.

AD 632 The prophet Muhammad, founder of Islam, dies at Medina in Arabia.

AD 768-814 Charlemagne unites central Europe in a single empire.

ROOTS OF CHINESE CIVILISATION: AD 960 – 1644

960 Zhao Kuangyin usurps the throne, founding the Song dynasty.

1115-1234 Jurched tribesmen from

Manchuria establish the Jin dynasty in much of northern China.

1272-9 The Mongols, under Genghis Khan's grandson Kublai, conquer southern China and establish the Yuan dynasty in 1280.

1275-91 The Venetian traveller Marco Polo serves in Kublai's court.

1368 The anti-Mongol leader Zhu Yuanzhang proclaims himself first emperor of the Ming dynasty.

1583 Jurched tribes in Manchuria appoint a new leader, Nurhachi.

PERFECT WARRIOR   A Persian artist painted this scene of Genghis Khan in his tent.

TEA TRADE   A Dutch ship bears the first cargo of tea for Europe.

1609 The Dutch East India Company takes its first shipment of tea from China to Europe.

1644 Manchu (Jurched) forces seize Beijing and complete the overthrow of the Ming dynasty – China's last native dynasty.

POWER AND WEALTH

61 An Academy of Painting is founded at Nanjing.

978-84 Scholars compile a major encyclopaedia in 1000 volumes.

1040 Movable type of baked clay is invented about this time.

1342 A papal legate, John of Marignolli, is received at the imperial court.

1400 Early versions of the novels, the *Romance of the Three Kingdoms* and *Water Margin* are published about this time.

1404-33 Seven Chinese expeditions, commanded by the eunuch Zheng He, voyage as far as the coast of East Africa.

1408 Some 2000 scholars complete the *Yongle dadian*, a mammoth work summarising the essential core of Chinese learning in 22 877 books.

1583-1610 The Italian Jesuit Matteo Ricci lives in China.

1603 The Donglin Academy is founded at Wuxi, Jiangsu province, to promote a conservative Confucianist revival in the declining days of the Ming dynasty.

1637 The scholar Song Yingxing's *Tiangong Kaiwu* summarises Chinese technology in encyclopaedic form.

NATURE'S MEANING   Mountains symbolised rugged endurance, willows a yielding graciousness. This scene was painted about 1200.

LEARNING, LIFESTYLE AND LEISURE

982 Viking settlers colonise Greenland.

1066 Norman conquest of England.

1099 The First Crusade captures Jerusalem.

1348-9 The Black Death – a world pandemic of plague.

1453 Ottoman armies capture Constantinople.

1456 The German Johann Gutenberg prints the Bible from movable type.

1492 The expulsion of the Moors from Granada

completes the Christian Reconquista (reconquest) of Spain.

1592-3 and 1597-8 The Japanese invade Korea.

1607 The first English settlement is founded in Virginia, at Jamestown.

1618-48 The Thirty Years' War, between Catholic and Protestant armies, ravages central Europe.

1620 The Pilgrim Fathers land at Plymouth Rock.

SUPPLICATION   Pope Gregory the Great leads a procession, praying for an end to the plague.

REST OF THE WORLD

CHINA UNDER THE QING: 1645 – 1735

POWER AND WEALTH

1644 The seven-year-old Fulin, son of the Manchu leader Abahai (who died in 1643), is the first emperor of the Qing dynasty – using the reign name Shunzhi. The effective ruler for the time being is the regent Dorgon, his uncle.

1652 Tibet's ruler and religious leader, the Dalai Lama, receives a splendid welcome in Beijing. He formally acknowledges the suzerainty of the Qing dynasty over his Himalayan realm.

FOUNDER The Shunzhi Emperor, first Qing ruler.

1662 The Shunzhi Emperor dies in his twenties of smallpox and is succeeded by a six-year-old son who assumes the reign name Kangxi. The Kangxi Emperor's 60-year reign will be one of the longest and most prosperous in Chinese history.

1673-81 A serious rebellion in southern China, the Three Feudatories revolt, is crushed by Manchu forces. The Qing dynasty has finally asserted its control over the south.

1683 Annexation of Taiwan, completing the Qing conquest of China.

1684 The British East India Company establishes itself in Guangzhou (Canton).

1689 Treaty of Nerchinsk settles Chinese-Russian border frictions.

1722 The Kangxi Emperor dies and is succeeded by his autocratic son, the Yongzheng Emperor.

1728 Treaty of Kiatkha regulates Russian-Chinese trade.

1735 Death of the Yongzheng Emperor.

LEARNING, LIFESTYLE AND LEISURE

ARTIST'S ALBUM Budding artists copied prints like this from the *Mustard Seed Garden Manual*, first published in 1679.

1669 The Kangxi Emperor issues an imperial 'precept' detailing moral principles for the guidance of Chinese village life.

1716 A dictionary of Chinese characters, commissioned by the Kangxi Emperor, lists some 42000 characters.

1717 After nine years spent surveying China, the Jesuits Pierre Jartoux, Jean-Baptiste Régis and others produce an atlas of the empire. They were entrusted with the task by the Kangxi Emperor, an enthusiastic patron of the Jesuits and of the learning and technology they brought from Europe.

1729 Opium-smoking is officially (and in the event ineffectually)

POISONED DREAMS The Victorian artist Thomas Allom painted this scene of Chinese opium smokers.

prohibited. Later prohibitions will be equally unavailing.

REST OF THE WORLD

ROYAL DEATH Charles I's execution, painted by an eyewitness.

1649 England's Civil War ends with victory for the Parliamentarians. King Charles I is executed.

1665 The English scientist Isaac Newton discovers the laws of gravity.

1701 Yale College is founded at Cambridge, Massachusetts.

1709 The Englishman Abraham Darby smelts iron with coked coal.

1710 The Meissen porcelain factory is founded in Saxony.

1715 The Sun King, Louis XIV of France, dies.

1717 George Frederick Handel's *Water Music* is first performed.

1719 Daniel Defoe's *Robinson Crusoe* is published.

MUSIC MAN The Messiah's composer George Frederick Handel modelled in terracotta.

CHINA UNDER THE QING: 1736 – 1798

1736 Accession of the Qianlong Emperor, succeeding his father the Yongzheng Emperor. He is in his mid-twenties and will reign for 60 years.

1774 A handsome, clever young army officer, He Shen, rises in the favour of the emperor. He dominates the Chinese government for the next two decades, hugely enriching himself in the process and encouraging the spread of corruption at all levels of society.

1787-8 A rising in Taiwan is suppressed.

1793-4 Lord Macartney leads a British diplomatic mission to China.

IMPERIAL REBUFF The British caricaturist James Gilray gave his view of Lord Macartney's reception in Beijing.

1793 Outbreak of the White Lotus rebellion, an attempt to restore China to native rule.

1796 The Qianlong Emperor abdicates out of respect for his grandfather the Kangxi Emperor – he does not want to exceed his grandfather's 60-year reign. He designates a son as his successor (reigning as the Jiaqing Emperor), but continues to exercise effective power until his death in 1799.

1736 China at the accession of the Qianlong Emperor is experiencing a period of remarkable prosperity which lasts until the later decades of the 18th century.

1740 The Imperial Household establishes its own acting troupe.

1745 The Qianlong Emperor, a dedicated patron of the arts, publishes 40 poems that he himself has composed in praise of a favourite palace near Beijing.

1750 Wu Jingzi's

STATUS SYMBOL An exquisitely embroidered silk square proclaims the rank and status of an important mandarin.

novel *The Scholars*, completed around this time, satirises official corruption and the state examination system.

1757 The importance of poetry is upgraded in official examinations.

1759 A new code regulating ceremonial dress is issued.

1766 Pu Songling's *Strange Tales from an Eccentric's Studio*, a collection of 445 short stories about the mysterious and supernatural, is published.

1772-88 A 'literary inquisition' leads to the destruction of more than 2000 works condemned on grounds of morality or security.

At the same time, the Qianlong Emperor commissions the massive *Siku quanshu* (*Complete Library of the Four Branches of Literature*) that will eventually run to 36 275 volumes.

1792 Cao Xueqin's novel *Hong lou meng* (*Dream of Red Mansions*) – widely regarded as one of the finest works of Chinese fiction – is published. It chronicles the decline of the once-powerful and wealthy Jia family and includes a huge cast of 30 principal characters and more than 400 minor ones.

AUSTRALIA ANNEXED Captain James Cook claims New South Wales for the British crown on August 23, 1770.

1763 The Seven Years' War ends, confirming British ascendancy in Canada and India.

1768 First edition of the *Encyclopaedia Britannica*.

1769-70 During his first circumnavigation of the globe, the Englishman Captain James Cook explores the east coast of Australia.

1776 The American Declaration of Independence.

HERO OF THE SEAS In 1798 Nelson destroyed a French fleet in the Battle of the Nile.

1785 The American Benjamin Franklin invents bifocal spectacles.

1788 The 'First Fleet' of convict ships arrives in Australia.

1789 The fall of the Bastille in Paris marks the start of the French Revolution.

1793 Louis XVI of France is executed. The metric system is introduced in France.

1796 The English doctor Edward Jenner discovers a smallpox vaccine.

CHINA UNDER THE QING: 1799 – 1860

POWER AND WEALTH

1799 On the death of the Qianlong Emperor, the Jiaqing Emperor has his father's corrupt favourite He Shen arrested and forces him to commit suicide. The new emperor tries to curb official corruption.

1816 Lord Amherst's diplomatic mission fails after he refuses to kowtow to the emperor.

1821 The Daoguang Emperor succeeds his father.

1839-42 First Opium War. The Chinese authorities attempt to stamp out the opium trade. British traders feel threatened and war results in which Britain defeats China and is ceded Hong Kong.

SETTLEMENT The 1842 Treaty of Nanjing closed the First Opium War.

1850-64 The Taiping rebellion, led by a failed examination candidate who claims to be Christ's younger brother, causes massive loss of life.

1851 The Xianfeng Emperor succeeds his father.

1856-60 Second Opium War.

LEARNING, LIFESTYLE AND LEISURE

1814 The first Chinese Protestant convert is baptised.

1822 A translation of the New Testament into Chinese is published.

SPREADING THE WORD
The need to translate the Bible into Chinese fostered missionary achievements in compiling grammars and dictionaries.

1838 The Medical Missionary Society, with backing from both the United States and Britain, is established in China.

1849 The first Chinese immigrants reach San Francisco. Over the next few decades California draws large numbers of Chinese seeking a better life there. By 1870 there are 56 000 Chinese in the United States, most of them living along the west coast.

1850 The English-language *North China Herald* is published in Shanghai.

1860 French and British troops burn the Yuan Ming Yuan summer palace.

GOLDEN GATEWAY
The gold fields lured thousands of Chinese immigrants to California.

REST OF THE WORLD

1801-3 Matthew Flinders circumnavigates Australia.

1803 The territory of the USA is virtually doubled by purchasing the Louisiana territory from France.

1804-6 Lewis and Clark explore the American West.

1805 Horatio Nelson destroys a French and Spanish fleet off Cape Trafalgar.

DEFEATED
Napoleon retreats from Moscow in 1812.

1815 Napoleon is defeated at Waterloo.

1845-6 Famine in Ireland provokes mass emigration.

1846-8 The USA annexes more territory after the Mexican war.

SLAVE AUCTION Slavery was not finally abolished in the British Empire until 1833.

1853 A US fleet, led by Commodore Matthew Perry, forces Japan to open up to foreign trade.

1854-6 Russia is defeated in the Crimean War.

1861 The Chinese government sets up a foreign ministry for the first time.

1862 The six-year-old Tongzhi Emperor succeeds his father. His mother, the Empress Dowager Ci Xi, gathers power into her hands until she becomes China's effective ruler.

1894-5 China is defeated by Japan in the Sino-Japanese War.

1898 The 100 Days reform movement, led by the pro-Western Confucian scholar Kang Youwei, is

MILITARY HUMILIATION Japan's Western-style army trounces the Chinese forces at Pingyang.

RIGHTEOUS RAGE Boxer rebels assassinate the German ambassador.

defeated by conservatives.

1900-1 The anti-Western Boxer rebellion.

1908 The Guangxu Emperor is succeeded by his two-year-old great-nephew Pu Yi.

1912 The Republic of China is proclaimed, marking the end of the Qing dynasty. The Zuantong Emperor (Pu Yi) abdicates – he will live until 1967.

POWER AND WEALTH

1861 The Beijing Language Institute, where Chinese students can learn Western languages, is founded.

1865 The China Inland Mission is established to bring Protestant Christianity to the interior.

1872 The first Chinese students are sent to USA to learn about Western techniques and technology.

1881 The Shanghai Telephone Company is established.

1895 The YMCA is established in China.

1896 The first moving-picture show is put on in Shanghai.

1897 The first modern bank is established in Shanghai.

1898 The Western-style Imperial University is established.

1902 The government issues an edict forbidding foot-binding.

1904 Soccer is introduced to China.

1905 Civil service examinations are abolished as they are now regarded as old-fashioned.

WOMAN'S LOT A rich lady, attended by a maid, reveals her tiny foot, the result of childhood binding.

LEARNING, LIFESTYLE AND LEISURE

1861-5 American Civil War.

1867 The USA buys Alaska from Russia for $7.2 million.

The British North American colonies confederate as Canada.

1868 The 'Meiji Restoration' in Japan sees the overthrow of the last dynasty of shoguns in the name of the emperor.

1869 The USA's first coast-to-coast railroad is completed.

1876 General Custer's command wiped out at the Battle of the Little Big Horn.

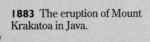

1883 The eruption of Mount Krakatoa in Java.

1889 Japan adopts a Western-style parliamentary constitution.

1895 X-rays are discovered. Guglielmo Marconi invents the wireless.

1911 The Norwegian explorer Roald Amundsen reaches the South Pole.

HAIL FREEDOM! Designed by Gustave Eiffel and dedicated in 1886, the Statue of Liberty was a gift from the French to the United States.

OVER THE SEA The French aviator Louis Blériot flies the English Channel on July 25, 1909.

REST OF THE WORLD

INDEX

156

ACKNOWLEDGMENTS

Abbreviations T = Top; M = Middle;
B = Bottom; R = Right; L = Left

AKG = Archiv für Kunst und Geschichte, London
BAL = Bridgeman Art Library, London
BM = The British Museum, London
ETA = ET Archive, London
MEPL = Mary Evans Picture Library, London
TBA = Toucan Books Archive, London
V&A = Victoria & Albert Museum, London

1 *Peiwenzhai Gengzhitu* early 18th century/BM. 2-3 Chinese painting on silk, late 18th century, V&A/BAL. 4 MEPL, TL; Christie's, London/BAL, ML; Chinese print, late 18th century, Philadelphia Free Library/BAL, MR. 5 Chinese painting on silk, 18th century, The Oriental Museum, Durham University/BAL, TL; Musée Guimet/Giraudon, TR; *Peiwenzhai Gengzhitu*, early 18th century/BM, BL; *Shanghai wheelbarrow*, 1870s, photograph John Thomson/The Mansell Collection, BR. 7 BAL, TR. 8 National Maritime Museum/ETA, BL; *Men using chain pump*, 1870s/The Mansell Collection, BR. 10-11 *Emperor Kang Shi's tour of Kiang-Han in 1699*, Chinese painting, British Library/BAL. 12 *Shepherdess with sheep*, porcelain dish, early 18th century, *Symbol for Yin-Yang*, ink on paper, The Oriental Museum, Durham University, BL, BR. 13 *Sages studying the Ying-Yang symbol*, painting on silk, BM, ML; *Taoist pendant*, Chinese 18th century, Private Collection/Werner Forman Archive, MR. 14 *The Kirghizes presenting horses to Chien Lung*, 18th-century scroll of Castiglione/ETA, T; *Christian mission in China*, 1880s/The Mansell Collection, B. 15 *Chinese family*, 1870s, Peabody Essex Museum, Salem. 16 *Courtyard in house of mandarin, Peking*, 1870s, photograph John Thomson. 17 *Filial piety*, woodblock from *Ershi si xiao*, 1688/British Library. 18 *Peiwenzhai Gengzhitu* early 18th century/BM, ML; Joint Publishing (Hong Kong) Company Limited, BR. 19 *Woman spinning*, 1870s, photograph John Thomson/Arthur Lockwood. 20 Illustration by Gill Tomblin. 21 *A Chinese bride and bridegroom*, anon, from *The Far East Albumen*, RPS05.5 BLA/The Royal Photographic Society Picture Library, TL; *Marriage ceremony*, Chinese painting, 19th century, V&A/ETA, BR. 22 Hulton Getty, T; *Chinese courtesan*, 1870s, Howard Ricketts Collection, London, B. 23 *Group of Chinese musicians*, 19th century, from export album (Or.7408), BM. 24 Illustration by Gill Tomblin. 25 *Peiwenzhai Gengzhitu* early 18th century/BM. 26 Illustration by Gill Tomblin. 27 *Coming of age*, Chinese embroidered hanging, 18th century, V&A/BAL. 28-29 *Emperor Kang Shi's tour of Kiang-Han in 1699*, Chinese painting, British Library/BAL. 30 *One-man puppet show*, 19th century from export album (Or.2262)/BM, BL; *The lesson*, photograph John Thomson, hand-tinted albumen, 1860s, Janet Lehr Inc, NY, TR. 32-33 Illustration by Paul Wright. 34 Illustration by Gill Tomblin. 35 *Family group of several generations of women*, anon, from *The Far East Albumen*, 05.5 BLA/The Royal Photographic Society Picture Library, T; *Geomancer's compass*, drawing by Kent Crane from *China in Sign and Symbol*, by Louise Crane, MM. 36 Illustration by Gill Tomblin. 37 *Portraits of the dead*, drawing by Louise Crane. 38-39 Illustration by Gill Tomblin. 41 Bonora/Giraudon, MR; Lauros/Giraudon, B. 42 *Monks in private grotto, Peking*, 1860s/Library of Congress. 43 *Taiping rebellion*, SOAS/ETA, ML; *Boxer Amulet*/AKG, MR. 44 MEPL, BL; Odile

Cavendish, London/BAL, BM; British Library/BAL, MM. 45 *Peiwenzhai Gengzhitu*, early18th century/BM. 46 BAL/Giraudon. 47 *Physic street, Canton*, 1860s, John Thomson/International Museum of Photography at George Eastman House, Rochester, TL; *Plan of city of Peking*, 1843, Bibliothèque Nationale Paris/ETA, BR. 48-49 Illustration by Gill Tomblin. 50 *Beggar*,1790s/V&A. 51 *Linchong's basket shop*,1820s, Chinese artist/Courtesy Hong Kong Bank Archives 52 Illustration by Gill Tomblin. 53 *Moneylender*, 19th century, Chinese watercolour, V&A/ETA, BL; *Merchant* 1790s, V&A, BM. 54 *Throwing porcelain on the wheel*, V&A. 55 *Potters decorating the wares*, 1637, woodblock print/British Library, T; *Chinese blue and white decorated bowl*, Christie's, London, BR. 56 *Boat*, pale green nephrite, 18th century, China/Eugene Fuller Memorial Collection, Seattle Art Museum, photograph Paul Macupia, T; *Strolling musicians*, Ku Chien Lung (Kokenro), 17th century, silk Kakemono, Museum of Fine Arts Boston, BR. 57 MEPL, T; Giraudon, M. 58 *Transporting opium*, 19th century Chinese painting on glass, V&A/ETA, ML; *Opium Den*, 1880s V&A, B. 59 *Brothel*, from *Dianshizhai*/British Library. 60-61 From *Peiwenzhai Gengzhitu*, early 18th century/BM, BR. 61 Giraudon, B. 62 Illustration by Gill Tomblin, BL. 63 Illustration by Gill Tomblin. 64 From *Peiwenzhai Gengzhitu*, early 18th century/BM. 65 Metropolitan Museum of Art, New York/Werner Forman Archive, TR; Philadelphia Free Library/Giraudon, BR. 66, 68 V&A. 69 *Nan-K'on Pass North of Peking* , 1919, photograph John Thomson/Private Collection. 70-71 *A Canton junk in Bay of Amoy*, 1860s, photograph John Thomson/Collection Bernd Lohse, Leverknsen, West Germany. 72-73 Illustration by Peter Morter. 74 From *Dianshizhai*/British Library. 76 V&A, TM, BL. 77 V&A, BL; *Beggars Foochow*, 1870s, photograph John Thomson/Hulton Getty, BR. 78 V&A. 79 Illustration by Gill Tomblin. 80 V&A, TR, BL. 81 *Empress Dowager, Tz'u-hsi and the Imperial Eunuchs*, 1900s, Yu, court photographer/Freer Gallery of Art, Smithsonian Institute, T; Private Collection/Werner Forman Archive, M; Illustration by Gill Tomblin, B. 82 Illustration by Gill Tomblin, BL; V&A, BR. 83 Giraudon, T; *Prince Kung*, 1870s, photograph John Thomson/Private Collection, BR. 84-85 *Gardens at Yuan Ming Yuan*, 18th century, Bibliothèque Nationale Paris/ETA. 85 V&A, BR. 86 *Workers on the Yangtze river*, 1870s, photograph John Thomson/Arthur Lockwood. 87 Illustration by Gill Tomblin, TR; ETA, BL. 88 *Page from a medical work on edibles* by Shen Lilong, 1691, BM, TR; Illustration by Gill Tomblin, B. 89 *Street doctor*, 1870s, photograph by John Thomson/Private Collection, TL; *Bronze acupuncture figurine*, Chinese 18th century/Science and Society Picture Library, TM; MEPL, BR. 90 *Suburban residents, Canton*, 1860s, photograph John Thomson, courtesy International Museum of Photography, George Eastman House, Rochester. 91 Illustration by Gill Tomblin. 92 BM, T; 92-93 *Bamboo raft on Ya river*, 1908, photograph E.H.Wilson/Photographic Archives of the Arnold Arboretum, Havard University. 94 TBA. 95 Joint Publishing (Hong Kong) Company Limited, BL; From *Peter Mundy's Sketches of China*, 1830s/Bodleian Library, Oxford, BR. 96 V&A/BAL. 97 V&A/ETA, TL; MEPL, MM; Detail from *Le Thé à l'Anglaise* , painting by M.B.Olivier, Château Versailles/Lauros/Giraudon, B. 98 *Beer and peanut hawker, Hong Kong*, 1860s, photograph John Thomson/Private Collection. 99 ETA. 100 Lauros/

Giraudon. 101 Bonara/Giraudon, TL; Bibliothèque Nationale, Paris/BAL, BR. 102-3 *View of Mount Wutai, Shanxi Province*, Bibliothèque Nationale/BAL. 104 *Priests and laymen at grave of Christian*, 1860s photograph M.A.Baptista/Essex Institute, Frederick T. Ward China Library, Salem. 105 *Porcelain brush pot*, late 18th century/The Oriental Museum, Durham University, BL; *Among green mountains I build a house*, 1663 by K'un-ts'an/Shanghai Museum, TR. 106 Illustration by Gill Tomblin, TL; Bibliothèque Nationale, Paris, TR. 107 MEPL. 108-9 Illustration by Gill Tomblin. 110 *Temple, Macao, China*, 1900s, photograph H.C.White/Library of Congress. 111 *Mosque in walled city of T'ao-chou, Kansu*, photograph Joseph F. Rock/Photographic Archives of the Arnold Arboretum, Harvard University. 112-13 Illustration by Gill Tomblin. 114 From *Dianshizhai*/British Library. 115 *Criminals awaiting execution*, 1900s, photograph E.H.Wilson/Photographic Archives of the Arnold Arboretum, Harvard University. 116 *Execution Scene*, 1860s/Library of Congress; From *Dianshizhai*/British Library, BL. 118 Bibliothèque Nationale, Paris/ETA. 119 From *Peter Mundy's sketches of China*, 1830s/Bodleian Library, Oxford. 120 Illustration by Gill Tomblin. 121 *The cage of death*, 1870s, photograph John Thomson/Arthur Lockwood. 122 *Opium Ships at Lin Tsin*, 1824, engraving by E.Duncan, National Maritime Museum, London/BAL, ML; From *Dianshizhai*/British Library , BR. 123 Palace Museum, Peking/ETA. 124-5 Private Collection/ETA. 126 ETA. 127 Illustration by Gill Tomblin. 128 Reproduced by permission of the Commercial Press (Hong Kong) Limited from the publication *Daily Life in the Forbidden City*, TM, TR. 129 MEPL. 130-1 Private Collection/ETA. 132 V&A, TR; *Arsenal at Nanking*, 1860s, photograph John Thomson/Arthur Lockwood. 133 Bibliothèque Nationale, Paris/BAL. 134 *The Empress Dowager in a palace courtyard, Peking*, 1908, Yu, court photographer/Photographic Archives of the Arnold Arboretum, Harvard University. 135 The Mansell Collection. 136-7 Illustration by Terence Dalley. 138 *Interior of a mandarin's house*, 1870s, photograph John Thomson/Arthur Lockwood. 139, 140 Illustrations by Gill Tomblin. 141 *Cantonese mandarin and his wife*, 1860s, photograph M.Miller/Royal Asiatic Society. 142 Arthur Lockwood, BL, BR. 143 Popperfoto, T; The Mansell Collection, B. 144 British Library. 145 *Ministers of the Foreign Office, Peking*, 1870s, photograph John Thomson/Arthur Lockwood. 146 Information Bank, David Wade, BL; David Allison, TR. 147 Shanghai Museum/The Asia Society Galleries, from *The Chinese Scholar's Studio; Artistic life in the Late Ming Period*, editors Chu-Tsing Li, James C.Y. Watt, publishers Thames and Hudson © 1987 The Asian Society Galleries, TL, BM; TBA, TR. 148 *Court in a mandarin's house*, 1870s, photograph John Thomson/Arthur Lockwood, TL; British Library, TR. 149 *Rice paddies and tea scrubs, hills of Kiangsi, South-East China*, 1902, Underwood and Underwood/Library of Congress. 150 BM/BAL, TL; Bibliothèque Nationale, Paris/BAL, TR; AKG, ML; BM/ETA, MR; *Crucifixion*, fresco by Duccio Di Buoninsegna, Dnomo, Sienna/BAL, BM. 151 Bibliothèque Nationale, Paris/BAL, TL; O'Shea Gallery, London/BAL, TR; *Zhang Shui Cheng*/BAL, MM; *Les Tres Riches Heures du Duc de Berry*, Musée Conde, Chantilly/Giraudon/BAL, BL. 152 Reproduced by permission of the Commercial Press (Hong Kong) Limited, from the publication *Daily Life in the Forbidden City*, T; British Library, ML; Stapleton Collection/BAL, MR;

Private Collection/BAL, BL; Fitzwilliam Museum, Cambridge/BAL, BR. 153 V&A/BAL, T; Private Collection/Werner Forman Archive, M; *Captain Cook taking possession of the Australian continent*, painting Samuel Calvert, National Library of Australia, Canberra/ BAL, BL; *Lord Horatio Nelson*, painting Sir William Beechey, Cider House Galleries Ltd., Bletchingley/BAL, BR. 154 National Maritime Museum/BAL, TR; MEPL, ML; Corbis/Bettmann, MR; Hulton Getty, BL; Corbis/Bettmann, BR. 155 MEPL, TL; AKG, TR, BL, BR; *Chinese woman and servant*, 1860s, attributed to John Thomson/TBA, MM.

Front cover: BAL, TL; V&A, TR; The Mansell Collection, ML; ETA, MM; Illustration by Gill Tomblin, MR; BAL, BL; Werner Forman Archive, BM; BM, BR.

Back cover: Photographic Archives of the Arnold Arboretum, Harvard University, TL; V&A, TR, MR; Janet Lehr Inc., New York, ML; BAL, BL, BR.

The publishers are grateful to the following individuals and publishers for their kind permission to quote passages from the publications below:

Princeton University Press from *The Adventures of Wu: The Cycle of Peking Man* by H.Y. Lowe, 1983.
Oxford University Press from *The Analects* by Confucius, translated by Raymond Dawson, 1993.
Penguin Books Ltd from *The Death of Woman Wang* by Jonathan D. Spence, 1979.
Penguin Books Ltd from *The Dream of the Red Chamber* by Cao Xuequin, translated by David Hawkes, 1973.
Allen and Unwin Ltd from *Yuan Mei: Eighteenth-Century Chinese Poet* by Arthur Waley, 1956.

59-018-1